PROCESSOR NETWORKS
AND ASPECTS OF THE MAPPING PROBLEM

Cambridge International Series on Parallel Computation: 2

PROCESSOR NETWORKS AND ASPECTS OF THE MAPPING PROBLEM

PETER A. J. HILBERS
Department of Mathematics and Systems Engineering
Shell Research, Amsterdam

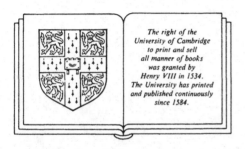

The right of the
University of Cambridge
to print and sell
all manner of books
was granted by
Henry VIII in 1534.
The University has printed
and published continuously
since 1584.

CAMBRIDGE UNIVERSITY PRESS

Cambridge

New York Port Chester Melbourne Sydney

CAMBRIDGE UNIVERSITY PRESS
Cambridge, New York, Melbourne, Madrid, Cape Town,
Singapore, São Paulo, Delhi, Tokyo, Mexico City

Cambridge University Press
The Edinburgh Building, Cambridge CB2 8RU, UK

Published in the United States of America by
Cambridge University Press, New York

www.cambridge.org
Information on this title: www.cambridge.org/9780521402507

First published 1991
First paperback edition 2011

A catalogue record for this publication is available from the British Library

ISBN 978-0-521-40250-7 Hardback
ISBN 978-1-107-40417-5 Paperback

Cambridge University Press has no responsibility for the persistence or
accuracy of URLs for external or third-party internet websites referred to in
this publication, and does not guarantee that any content on such websites is,
or will remain, accurate or appropriate. Information regarding prices, travel
timetables, and other factual information given in this work is correct at
the time of first printing but Cambridge University Press does not guarantee
the accuracy of such information thereafter.

To Pauline,
Pim,
Jelle,
and Job

Contents

Preface

As small processors become increasingly cheaper, it becomes increasingly attractive to use them simultaneously in solving a single problem. At least three correlated issues have to be addressed to make this attractiveness turn into acceptance. The first one is how these processors should be organized to solve problems efficiently. The second issue concerns the developments of methods to decompose problems into parts that can efficiently be run in parallel. The distribution of these parts over the available processors is the third issue.

In this work we present a rather fundamental treatment of topics related to the first and the last issue. The second issue concerning parallel programming is undoubtedly of vital importance. The subject, however, is far from being understood well at the moment of writing, and is an area of extensive research. Despite this, I have tried to incorporate the relevant aspects. Chapter 1 is an introduction to the field of distributed computing. Since graph theory is heavily used, in Chapter 1 a brief introduction to graph theory with special attention to processor networks is also presented. Chapter 2 is devoted to aspects of the price/performance of processor networks. In Chapter 3 a new class of processor networks, which have an excellent price–performance ratio, is introduced. Chapter 4 is devoted to a method by which homogeneous distributions of work over processors can be obtained. In Chapter 5 this method is applied to an important class of parallel programs and an important class of processor networks. Chapter 6 considers examples of distributions for the processor networks introduced in Chapter 3. Finally, in Chapter 7 the routing of messages within a processor network is considered. In a slightly different form this chapter has been published as article in Distributed Computing. Most of the material presented in this work also appeared in my Ph.D. thesis. The subject, however, deserves a more extensive introduction. I hope that I have been able to explain my thoughts sufficiently clearly.

While it is intended mainly for computer scientists, others interested in (future) processor networks or homogeneous distributions may find the book useful. Graduate students in computer science who have had some previous experience with parallel programming will find it valuable.

Several people have helped me during the years while I was doing my research at the university of Groningen. First of all, I thank my promoter Jan van de Snepscheut for his encouragement, cooperation, and helpful comments. It has been a privilege to work under his guidance. Helpful comments were also made by Wim Hesselink, Johan Lukkien, Martin Rem, Jan Tijmen Udding, and Gert Vegter. The management of Koninklijke/Shell-Laboratorium, Amsterdam is given grateful acknowledgement for giving me the opportunity to write this book. Last but not least I want to thank my colleagues, especially Klaas Esselink, for their assistance in my producing this work.

Chapter 1

Introduction

There is and there always will be a demand for faster and bigger computers. The current answer to this demand is: Use many processors simultaneously in solving one problem. A large variety of such multiprocessor systems have been developed in recent years. Those multiprocessor systems can be roughly divided into two classes: shared memory and non-shared memory systems. To the first class, the shared memory systems, very succesful members belong as Crays, Convexes, and Alliants. Their success is to a large extent the result of the ease with which existing software for sequential machines can be implemented on it. They, however, have one great flaw: enlarging the number of processors inevitably leads to memory contention problems.

Since drastic improvements in performance are not foreseen for the shared memory systems, another type of computer architectures is becoming more and more important and popular: the non-shared memory multiprocessor systems. Each processor has its own private store and interaction between processors takes place via the exchange of messages over a communications network. Such systems, which we call processor networks, were until recently mainly found at universities. Nowadays there are also commercially available processor networks such as ncubes and transputer networks.

It seems natural to use these systems for the implementation of so-called distributed algorithms, i.e., programs consisting of a collection of processes that communicate and synchronize via the exchange of messages. The design of provably correct distributed algorithms, however, is a difficult task. So we strive for methods to alleviate the design task. We therefore suggest separating the design of a distributed algorithm from its implementation on a processor network. This separation has several advantages.

- When, in the design, one has to consider the structure, i.e., the size and the topology, of the processor network on which the algorithm is to be executed the design task is unnecessarily complicated. Besides, the correctness of an algorithm should be independent of a processor network. Furthermore, the amount of parallelism of an algorithm usually depends on the problem size. For instance, multiplying two 3×3 matrices offers less possibility for parallelism than multiplying two 100×100 matrices.

- The complexity of an algorithm can be analysed without being influenced by typical features of the system on which the program is to be run. Consequently, quantities such as speedup, efficiency, and isoefficiency ([Woo 89]) can be determined in general terms.

- Another advantage is that it introduces the possibility of creating and destroying processes during the execution of an algorithm, and so the potential parallelism of an algorithm is not fixed beforehand but is determined dynamically, according to the needs of the computation. Consequently, the number of processes can be much larger than the actual number of processing nodes. At first glance this might seem to make the implementation of such algorithms very problematic. But the only way to formulate programs as a large number of communicating processes seems to be to introduce some kind of regularity. Or, as M. Rem ([Rem 79]) stated in 1979: 'A hierarchy is the only way to build complex systems with a high confidence level. They enjoy the nice property that we can prove assertions about the system by recursion over the hierarchy: assuming that the assertion holds for the subprocess we can prove that it holds for the process itself.' Therefore, we assume that the processes are similar and that they are arranged as a regular structure for which inductive arguments can be used. Typically, such structures are lines (arrays), trees, and meshes (matrices). Since these structures are commonly used in the field of sequential programming, the gap between sequential and distributed programming might become smaller.

Separating the design of a distributed algorithm from its implementation is only attractive when distributed algorithms can efficiently be implemented on a processor network. In Chapters 2 and 3 we analyse which properties a processor network should possess to be suitable as an implementation network and introduce a new class of interesting processor networks. An implementation of a collection of communicating processes on a processor network has at least two objectives. A first objective is to distribute processes over processors evenly. A second objective is to map two communicating processes onto processors that are not too far apart. In Chapters 4 to 6 we consider both objectives. Moreover, in Chapter 7 we also look at another problem associated with communications, viz. the deadlock-free routing of messages.

Throughout this book we consider neither any specific processor network nor any specific programming language. More specifically, we have tried to abstract from any irrelevant detail so that most of our work can be applied to any processor network and any programming language. For instance, the design of a distributed algorithm is to a large extent independent of the programming language in which the algorithm eventually has to be coded. For the mapping problem it, similarly, is not relevant how powerful a processor is.

1.1 Notions and notations

This section is devoted to notions and notations we use throughout this monograph.

A slightly unconventional notation for variable binding constructs is used, which is explained here informally.

Universal quantification is denoted by

$$\forall(l : D : E),$$

where $\forall$ is the quantifier, l is a list of bound variables, D is a predicate, and E is the quantified expression. Both D and E will, in general, contain variables from l. D delineates the domain of the bound variables. Existential quantification is denoted in a similar way with quantifier $\exists$. The number of solutions of the equation $l : D \wedge E$ is denoted by

$$\mathbf{N}(l : D : E).$$

For predicate D and expression E of type *real* the expression

$$\mathbf{S}(l : D : E)$$

denotes the sum over all values of E obtained by substituting for all variables in l values that satisfy D. For an integer function $f(l)$ we denote the maximum and minimum of f on D by

$$\mathbf{MAX}(l : D : f(l)) \text{ and } \mathbf{MIN}(l : D : f(l)),$$

respectively. By convention we have

$$\mathbf{MAX}(l : false : f(l)) = -\infty \text{ and } \mathbf{MIN}(l : false : f(l)) = \infty.$$

In the case of set formation we write

$$\{l : D : E\}$$

to denote the set of all values of E obtained by substituting for all variables in l values such that D holds. When obvious from the context the domain D is omitted.

A proposition of the form $E \Rightarrow G$ will often be proved in two or more steps by the introduction of one or more intermediate expressions. For instance, by proving $E = F$ and $F \Rightarrow G$, for some judiciously chosen expression F, we can prove $E \Rightarrow G$. This is recorded as follows.

$$
\begin{array}{ll}
& E \\
= & \{ \text{ hint why } E = F \} \\
& F \\
\Rightarrow & \{ \text{ hint why } F \Rightarrow G \} \\
& G
\end{array}
$$

The hint "calculus" indicates that an appeal to everyday mathematics, like predicate calculus or arithmetic, is meant. The above notations have been adopted from [Dijk90].

Next we give some notation from set theory. The number of elements in a finite set A is denoted by $|A|$. The cartesian product of two sets A and B, denoted by $A \times B$, is the set $\{a, b : a \in A \wedge b \in B : (a, b)\}$. So the cartesian product of A and B is the set of the ordered 2-tuples.

Next a long sequence of definitions from graph theory follows. These definitions are standard apart from notation (see [Berg73, Hara69]).

An undirected *graph* G is defined to consist of a nonempty set $G.V$ of vertices and a set $G.E$ of doubleton sets, which have two distinct vertices from G as elements. The elements of $G.E$ are called edges. Since all our graphs are undirected, the term undirected is omitted. Notice that an edge from a vertex to itself is not allowed in the definition of the edge set.

In general a vertex is not connected to all other vertices. Consequently, going from one vertex to another may require a sequence of edges. A *path* of length n, $n \geq 0$, of G is a sequence $v(i : 0 \leq i \leq n)$ of vertices such that

$$
\forall(i : 0 \leq i < n : \{v(i), v(i+1)\} \in G.E).
$$

Notice that a path of length 0 consists of a single vertex. A graph is called connected if every pair of vertices is joined by a path. Unless stated otherwise we assume a graph to be connected.

The *distance* $k(u, v)$ between two vertices u and v is the length of a shortest path between u and v. Notice that k is the unique function from $G.V \times G.V$ to $\mathbb{N}$ satisfying

(0) $k(u, v) = 0 \equiv u = v,$
(1) $\{v, x\} \in G.E \Rightarrow k(u, v) \le k(u, x) + 1 ,$
(2) $0 < k(u, v) \Rightarrow \exists (x : \{v, x\} \in G.E : k(u, v) \ge k(u, x) + 1),$

for all vertices u, v, and x of $G.V$.

The *diameter* k_G of graph G is the smallest integer such that every pair of vertices is joined by a path of length at most that integer:

$$k_G = \textbf{MAX}(u, v : u, v \in G.V : k(u, v)).$$

The *degree* $d(u)$ of vertex u is the number of edges containing u:

$$d(u) = \textbf{N}(e : e \in G.E : u \in e).$$

The degree d_G of G is:

$$d_G = \textbf{MAX}(u : u \in G.V : d(u)).$$

A graph is called *degree-regular* if all vertices have the same degree.

Three examples of graphs are the linear array, the ring, and the complete graph. A *linear array graph* is a graph $P(n)$ with

$$P(n).V = \{i : 0 \le i < n : i\} \text{ and } P(n).E = \{i : 0 \le i < n - 1 : \{i, i+1\}\}.$$

For a positive integer n we define the *ring graph* $R(n)$ by

$$R(n).V = \{i : 0 \le i < n : i\}, \text{ and}$$

$$R(n).E = \{i : 0 \le i < n : \{i, (i+1) \textbf{ mod } n\}\},$$

and in the *complete graph* $K(n)$ all vertices are connected to each other:

$$K(n).V = \{i : 0 \le i < n : i\}, \text{ and}$$

$$K(n).E = \{i, j : 0 \le i < j < n : \{i, j\}\}.$$

Notice that in $P(n)$ the degree of vertex 0 and vertex $n - 1$ is 1, while the other vertices have degree 2. In the graphs $R(n)$ and $K(n)$ all vertices have degree 2 and $n - 1$, respectively. Ring graphs and complete graphs are examples of degree-regular graphs. The diameter of $P(n)$, $R(n)$, and $K(n)$ is, for $n > 1$, $n - 1$, n **div** 2, and 1, respectively.

A processor network is viewed as a graph, called the implementation graph, in which the vertices are the processors and the edges are the links between the processors. All the above notions can, thus, be applied to processor networks.

We proceed with some notions that do not appear in the standard literature, but that are important for processor networks.

The *distance density function* of a graph G is the function $dk : G.V \times \mathbb{N} \to \mathbb{N}$ defined by

$$dk(x, i) = \mathbf{N}(y : y \in G.V : k(x, y) = i).$$

Hence, for a vertex x and a natural number i, $dk(x, i)$ denotes the number of vertices at distance i from x. Notice that for arbitrary graphs this number may depend on the vertex under consideration.

Graph G is called *distance-regular* if

$$\forall(x, y, i : x, y \in G.V \wedge i \in \mathbb{N} : dk(x, i) = dk(y, i)).$$

Notice that a distance-regular graph is degree-regular.

The *average distance* of graph G is defined by

$$\overline{k}_G = \frac{\mathbf{S}(x, y : x, y \in G.V : k(x, y))}{|G.V|^2}.$$

The calculation of the average distance of an arbitrary graph is hard. But, when G is distance-regular, the calculation is simpler. From

$\quad G$ is distance-regular
$= \quad \{ \text{ calculus } \}$
$\quad \forall(x, y : x, y \in G.V : \mathbf{S}(z : z \in G.V : k(x, z)) = \mathbf{S}(z : z \in G.V : k(y, z)))$

we conclude that

$$\mathbf{S}(x, y : x, y \in G.V : k(x, y))$$
$$= \quad \{ \text{ calculus } \}$$
$$\mathbf{S}(x : x \in G.V : \mathbf{S}(y : y \in G.V : k(x, y))$$
$$= \quad \{ \text{ see above } \}$$
$$|G.V| \cdot \mathbf{S}(y : y \in G.V : k(x, y))$$

for every $x \in G.V$, and, hence,

$$\overline{k}_G = \frac{\mathbf{S}(y : y \in G.V : k(x, y))}{|G.V|},$$

for every $x \in G.V$.

An example of a distance-regular graph is a ring graph $R(n)$. For even n we have $\overline{k}_{R(n)} = n^2 \mathbf{div} 4$.

Ring graphs and complete graphs are simple examples of so-called starred polygons, which are defined as follows. A *Hamiltonian cycle* of graph G is a path $v(i : 0 \le i \le n)$ such that $v(0) = v(n)$, $|G.V| = n$, and $\forall(g : g \in G.V : \exists(i : 0 \le i < n : g = v(i)))$. A *starred polygon* is a graph G containing a Hamiltonian cycle $v(i : 0 \le i \le n)$ such that for all m, where $0 \le m < n$,

$$\exists(i : 0 \le i < n : \{v(i), v((i+m) \bmod n)\} \in G.E)$$
$$\equiv$$
$$\forall(i : 0 \le i < n : \{v(i), v((i+m) \bmod n)\} \in G.E) .$$

Although the notion of Hamiltonicity of a graph seems to be of minor importance, when mappings of algorithms are considered, Hamiltonian cycles are extensively used.

Chapter 2

Processor networks

In this chapter we examine some aspects of the cost and performance of computer architectures whose designs are inspired by VLSI technology. First some characteristics of VLSI technology are considered. Next we discuss which properties a processor network should have in order to be suitable as an implementation graph for the distributed algorithms we are interested in. Then the cost–performance ratio of a processor network is globally analysed. We end with some criteria for processor networks.

2.1 Some characteristics of VLSI technology

Traditionally, computers were organized as a single processor, a large store, and a communication channel connecting them. The cost of the components employed to realize the processor was relatively high compared to the cost of wires connecting the components. Our first objective is to show that due to the advances in VLSI technology communication is nowadays more expensive than logic (see [Dall89, Seit84]).

- Communication is expensive in chip area.

  Most of the area of a chip is usually covered with wires on several layers, whereas transistors are found in the lowest layers only, and rarely take up more than about five per cent of the area.

- Communication is expensive in power.

  The energy dissipated by a switching event is almost entirely used to charge the capacitance of the node being switched. In most VLSI systems the capacitance of internal and interchip wires dominates device gate capacitance, and, hence, most of the energy is used to drive wires.

- Communication is expensive in speed, both internally and between chips.

Due to the relative high parasitic capacitance of a wire, the time it takes to propagate a signal through a wire is long compared with the switching time of a transistor. The propagation time depends on the length of a wire. For very short wires the delay scales logarithmically with wire length until a technology dependent length is reached. Beyond this length propagation time grows linearly with wire length.

Hence VLSI systems will be fast and efficient only when communication is local. In particular, this means that it is more attractive to construct systems consisting of a large collection of small processors each with its own small private store rather than one large processor with a large store. Moreover, systems with point-to-point links, each of which connects two processors, are preferred to systems with buses, each of which connects a large number of processors.

The principle of locality is particularly important since through the continuing evolution of technology circuits become smaller and smaller. When all physical dimensions and voltages are reduced by the same factor, the delay in short wires is also reduced by that factor. The delay in long wires, however, is not reduced. In long wires the delay is dominated by diffusive propagation of signals and is determined by the wire's RC product. While the capacitance C is scaled down linearly, the resistance R is scaled up linearly. Consequently, the delay is unaffected. We might also add that long wires do not benefit from reducing the feature size and should therefore be avoided where possible.

Size reduction also allows more circuitry to be implemented on the same amount of semiconductor material. In order to avoid long wires it seems preferable to incorporate multiple processors plus their private stores in a single chip rather than one single more complex processor. There is yet another strong argument for preferring multiple processors on a single chip. Most of the complexity of a VLSI system is at the chip level. The much coarser design rules of off-chip technology do not allow many wires to be routed away from a chip. Hence VLSI systems are limited by the wire density of the off-chip connections, and not by the number of on-chip connections. This situation will become even worse, as progress in off-chip technology continues to be slower than in on-chip technology.

From the above analysis we conclude that in an efficient VLSI system communication must be kept local and the number of interconnections must be kept small. Examples of such systems are transputer networks and small ncubes.

Another important characteristic of VLSI systems concerns regularity and replication. Regularity and replication both simplify the design of a network and reduce the costs of fabrication and maintenance. Consequently, it is preferable to have a large collection of small, identical processors together with a sparse, regular interconnection pattern. An additional advantage of such large systems is that they are extensible in the number of processors, and open-ended in performance. They can be expanded to be as large as desired with each part still operating at the same rate as when it is incorporated into a smaller system. This fortunate situation is absent in centralized systems.

2.2 Distributed computations

In the previous section we analysed the desired properties of a processor network from the hardware point of view. Next we look at the relevant issues of the distributed algorithms we shall be considering in the context of an implementation on a VLSI processor network.

As in [Mart80] we consider a distributed computation, i.e., the execution of a distributed algorithm, as a possibly varying set of processes that are connected by channels. A process is a computation described by a sequential program and by communication actions on channels. Processes do not share variables, but communicate with each other via the exchange of messages. Processes may be created and destroyed according to the needs of the computation. One further abstraction, which we use extensively, is to regard a distributed computation as a possibly varying graph, called the computation graph, in which the vertices are processes and the edges are channels.

As motivated in the previous chapter the kind of distributed algorithms that we are interested in are algorithms in which the number of processes far exceeds the number of processors of the network the algorithm is to be executed on. In order to be manageable those processes are arranged in some regular structure. Examples of such algorithms are distributed recursive algorithms, high-dimensional matrix algorithms, and many graph algorithms. When formulating programs as large collections of communicating processes interesting implementation issues arise. By the distribution of processes over the processor network, each processor will have been assigned many processes. Consequently, the time that a processor would otherwise be idle on account of communication latency can be filled by its executing different processes, provided the processors do not have to spend too much time in communication. This might imply that any implementation strategy which guarantees that enough processes are assigned to a processor could be used. It seems likely that this advantage strongly compensates the extra difficulties of intraprocessor scheduling, process administration, etc.

From these observations some important consequences for the implementation of such distributed algorithms on processor networks can be derived.

- It is desirable that the processor network have a regular structure. Mapping a regular structure efficiently on an irregular structure might even be impossible. Certainly it leads to computational behaviour which is difficult to analyse. Similar arguments can be applied to argue that the processors be identical.

- The structure of the processor network should be independent of the actual number of processors. In order to find general mapping strategies it is recommendable that only the topology and not the size of the processor network influence the implementation method. This has the additional advantage that when the network is expanded the implementation method need not be changed.

- The processor network should facilitate mappings for some standard computation graphs like lines, trees and meshes.

- A processor should have a separate routing unit. In order to avoid the processors' spending too much time in communication, it is preferred that computation and communication be done in parallel. For instance, the new transputer, the T9000, that has been announced for 1991 will indeed have a separate routing unit.

- The processor network should have a high throughput and a low latency. Since we strive for programs with a large number of processes, the processes and the size of the messages they are exchanging will, in general, be small, and the number of messages will be large. In order to obtain efficient implementations, the delivery of messages should be fast. That is, the time needed to deliver a single message in isolation in the processor network, called the latency of the network, must be short, and the total number of messages that can be handled per time unit, called the throughput of the network, must be large. When high throughput and low latency conflict, the former should be preferred.

Both latency and throughput are strongly dependent on the number of links per processor, the total number of processors, the length of the path a message must follow to arrive at its destination, and the routing strategy. In the next section these aspects are considered in more detail.

2.3 About the performance of a processor network

Both analyses in the previous two sections were rather qualitative. In reasoning about the performance of a processor network a more formal approach is necessary. In this section we first give a general analysis of the performance of a processor network. Then we consider the consequences of restricting ourselves to the class of distributed algorithms described in the previous section.

Usually processor networks are analysed by considering the number of processors, the degree, the diameter, the routing strategy, and the expansibility. As we have seen in section 2.1 two other parameters, viz. the width and the delay of a link, may not be disregarded. Under the assumption of equal links, high degree networks are strongly favored. High degree networks require, in general, more and longer wires than small degree ones. Hence, in a comparison both wire density and wire length have to be considered.

Our approach is based on the work of W.J. Dally([Dall89]) in which both factors are considered. A detailed analysis of the embedding of k-ary n-cubes into the plane is presented there. In order to have a general analysis we prefer to abstract as much as reasonable from a layout, and we make a slight modification to Dally's approach. To that end we define the bisection width of an arbitrary graph.

For a graph G and sets S, T, with $S, T \subseteq G.V$, the set $E(S, T)$ is given by

$$E(S,T) = \{s,t : s \in S \wedge t \in T \wedge \{s,t\} \in G.E : \{s,t\}\}.$$

The *bisection width* B of a graph G is defined by

$$B = \mathbf{MIN}(S,T : S \cup T = G.V \wedge ||S| - |T|| \leq 1 : |E(S,T)|).$$

Hence, the bisection width of a graph denotes the minimal number of edges between two almost equal-sized sets that partition the set of vertices of the graph. Determining the bisection width of an arbitrary graph is in general difficult. It can even be shown that the problem "Given a graph G and a positive integer n, is the bisection width of G at most n" is *NP*-complete (see [Even79]). Due to the importance of the bisection width in VLSI complexity theory, good bisection width lower bounds are known for a large variety of processor networks. In the following example, which is partly due to W.J. Dally [Dall89], the bisection width of a k-ary n-cube is given.

Example 2.1

The *k-ary n-cube* is the graph $C(k,n)$ with k^n vertices. A vertex has an n-digit radix-k address and has an edge with those vertices whose addresses differ from it by 1 in only one digit. The graph $C(2,n)$ is known as the boolean n-cube, the graph $C(k,2)$ as a torus, and the graph $C(k,1)$ is isomorphic to the ring graph $R(k)$. For the sake of convenience we assume both k and n to be even. The bisection width of $C(k,n)$ is $2 \cdot k^{n-1}$, for $k \neq 2$, and 2^{n-1}, for $k = 2$.
(End of example)

As might be concluded from this example two processor networks with the same number of processors differ in general in bisection width. As motivated in the previous section when two such processor networks are compared wire density must be held constant. To obtain the same wire density, we vary the width W of the links such that $B \cdot W = N$ for processor networks with N processors.

The impact of link width on the latency of a processor network becomes clear when we consider the transmission time of a message, which depends on the routing strategy used. Let L be the message length, W the width of a link, T_c the link delay, and n the number of links a message must traverse in order to arrive at its destination. Two general routing strategies are store-and-forward routing and wormhole routing.

When with store-and-forward routing a message is sent from source to destination via one or more intermediate processors, the message is first received at each intermediate processor in its entirety, and then it is transmitted to the next processor. The transmission time for a single message over one link is

$$\frac{L}{W} \cdot T_c.$$

Hence the total transmission time for a message that has to traverse n links is

$$n \cdot \frac{L}{W} \cdot T_c.$$

With *wormhole routing* a message is broken down in flits, the smallest unit of information a link can accept or refuse. Only the header flit of a message contains routing information. As soon as a processor examines the header flit of a message and a free outgoing link has been selected by the routing algorithm, the processor begins forwarding flits down that link. As flits are forwarded the message becomes spread out across the links on the path between the source and the destination of the message. Because only the header flit contains routing information, the flits in a message must remain in contiguous links of the network and cannot be interleaved with the flits of other messages, and only the last flit can release a link. Wormhole routing thus results in a transmission time for a single message that has to traverse n links of

$$(\frac{L}{W} + (n-1)) \cdot T_c.$$

Using wormhole routing the transmission time is reduced. Wormhole routing, to be used efficiently, requires a separate routing unit within each processor. Since a message becomes spread out over a path of links, all processors on the path are otherwise simultaneously occupied with the transmission of the message. This synchronization of processors leads in general to a decrease in performance.

From the transmission time $(\frac{L}{W} + (n-1)) \cdot T_c$ for a message which has to traverse n channels, W.J. Dally derives the following formula for the network latency, when wormhole routing is used:

$$T = (\frac{L}{W} + \bar{k}) \cdot T_c,$$

where $\bar{k}$ is the average network distance. The term $\bar{k}$ may not be the right component to express the average number of links a message has to traverse. The average number of links a message has to traverse depends on the routing algorithm that is used. By taking $\bar{k}$ one assumes that a shortest path routing algorithm is applied. In order to handle arbitrary routing algorithms we use the following definition for the *latency* of a network.

$$T = (\frac{L}{W} + \overline{RA}) \cdot T_c,$$

where $\overline{RA}$ denotes the average length of a path when routing algorithm RA is used.

Example 2.2
In this example we calculate the latency of a k-ary n-cube with 2^m vertices (see example 2.1). We thereby assume that shortest path routing algorithms are used. From example 2.1 and the assumption $B \cdot W = 2^m$ we derive $W = 2$ for a boolean n-cube, and $W = \frac{k}{2}$ for a k-ary n-cube with $k > 2$. The average distance of a k-ary n-cube is given by the following formula (see L.D. Wittie [Witt81])

$$\overline{RA} = n \cdot \frac{k^2 \text{ div } 4}{k}.$$

Hence, for a k-ary n-cube with 2^m vertices we have

$$T = (\frac{L}{2} + \frac{n}{2}) \cdot T_c, \quad \text{for } k = 2,$$

and
$$T = (\frac{2L}{k} + \frac{k \cdot n}{4}) \cdot T_c, \quad \text{for } k > 2.$$

For instance, assuming $T_c = 1$, $L = 128$, and $m = 12$, the latency of a boolean 12-cube is 70, of an 8-ary 4-cube 40, and for a 64-ary 2-cube(torus) the latency is 36.
(End of example)

From this example, which is corrected from [Dall89], we conclude that when link delay is constant, small degree networks achieve lower latency than large degree ones. When link delay depends on link length, latency favors small degree networks even more, since networks with a large degree require more and longer links than small degree networks. The main reason for this difference in latency is that by keeping wire cost constant large degree networks with narrow links are compared with small degree networks with wide links.

Another important metric of network performance is throughput. It is defined as the total number of bits the network can handle per time unit. We restrict ourselves to two methods proposed for estimating the throughput. Both methods assume a uniform distribution of messages over the links of the network. First we describe the methods. Thereafter we show that the difference between the methods concerns the link width.

The first method of estimating throughput (see [Dall89]) is to calculate the *network capacity nc* per processor. It is defined as the average bandwidth out of a processor divided by the average network distance:

$$nc = \frac{\overline{d} \cdot W}{\overline{k}},$$

where $\overline{d} = \frac{S(x::d(x))}{N}$. Notice that for degree-regular graphs $d = \overline{d}$ holds. Since wire density is held constant, the network capacity per node will not differ much for two networks with the same number of processors. Typically the throughput is some fraction of the network capacity per processor. After introducing the second method we will see which fraction it is.

The second method of estimating throughput is to calculate the *average message density per link* (see [Witt81]). For graph G the average message density per link, denoted by $\overline{md}$, is

$$\overline{md} = \frac{\overline{k} \cdot |G.V|}{|G.E|}.$$

Next we compare the two methods. The first result is due to Euler.

Property 2.3
For each graph G we have $\mathbf{S}(x : x \in G.V : d(x)) = 2 \cdot |G.E|$.
(End of property)

Property 2.4
For each graph G we have $nc \cdot \overline{md} = 2 \cdot W$.
(End of property)

Hence, when wire density is considered, two networks with the same capacity per processor have the same average bit density per link $\frac{\overline{md}}{W}$. The two methods are thus equivalent.

Example 2.5
Let G be a k-ary n-cube with 2^m vertices. Then we have $\overline{d} = 2n$, for $k > 2$, and $\overline{d} = n$, for $k = 2$. According to example 2.2 we find, both for $k > 2$ and for $k = 2$, $nc = 4$. Hence when comparing two k-ary n-cubes the increase in the average number of messages per link is compensated by the increase in the link width.
(End of example)

In some processor networks traffic is not uniformly distributed over the links of the network. A standard example is a tree network in which the links at the root have to account for a large portion of the total network traffic. In those cases it is preferable to estimate throughput by calculating the message traffic on each link instead of the average message density per link. One method that can be applied is to consider the situation in which each processor sends a message to each of the other processors, and then to calculate for each individual link the total number of messages that pass through that link. We shall not go into this.

We end this section with some conclusions about the performance of a processor network considered in the context of the class of distributed algorithms described in section 2.2. When we have a large collection of processes arranged as a regular structure, there is reasonable hope that message traffic is uniformly distributed over the links of the network. In that case small degree networks are preferred, since they achieve lower latency than large degree networks and equal throughput, provided wire density is held constant. The main reason is that by keeping wire density constant small degree networks have wide links. This greater bandwidth has as an additional advantage that it makes small degree networks less sensitive for non-uniform traffic than large degree networks with narrow links (see [Dall89]).

2.4 Some criteria for processor networks

Having identified the relevant issues we can now list several criteria for processor networks. We assume that the network is a large collection of small, identical processors with a regular interconnection pattern, that each processor has its own private store, and that each processor has a separate routing unit.

- The structure of the network should be independent of the size of the network.

- The network should facilitate efficient and simple mappings for lines, trees, and meshes.

- The network should have a simple routing algorithm.

- The network should have a low latency and a high throughput.

It is difficult to weigh the above criteria against each other. For instance, a large degree network offers more possibilities for mappings of trees than a small degree network, whilst a small degree network with wide links achieves a lower latency than a large degree network with narrow links. To take advantage of both situations the best choice might be to have a medium degree processor network with medium wide links.

Chapter 3

A new operation on graphs

In this chapter we introduce a new operation, called braiding, on graphs. Braiding is a ternary operation. It has two graphs and a function as operands, and the result is a graph. The following observations indicate that the braid operation might be useful as a construction method for VLSI processor networks.

- By choosing an appropriate function several properties of the two graphs, on which the braid operation is applied, are preserved. These properties include connectedness, degree-regularity, simple routing algorithms, and vertex-transitivity. Moreover, when a braid operation is applied on two small degree, regularly connected graphs, the result is a small degree graph with a regular interconnection pattern.

- As we have argued in the preceding chapter, when multiple processors on a single chip become feasible, on-chip links will have to be distinguished from off-chip links. The braid operation offers a means of discrimination. The result of a braid operation on two graphs may be viewed as a processor network with the on-chip links described by one graph and the off-chip links by the other graph.

- Braiding is applicable to arbitrary graphs. Hence braid operations can be applied consecutively to obtain a large, hierarchically constructed, processor network. Recently, several methods from graph theory have been proposed as strategies for interconnection networks (see [Berm86]). Since the purpose of these methods is, given a fixed degree and a fixed diameter, to construct a graph with as large a number of vertices as possible, attention is restricted to certain classes of graphs and issues like routing algorithm and average distance are not addressed. By applying the braid operation, highly symmetrical graphs with a simple routing algorithm and with a large but not maximal number of vertices can be constructed.

3.1 Braiding

In this section the braid operation is defined and some general properties of braid graphs are given. First some additional notations from set and graph theory are introduced.

The *cartesian product of graphs* G and U is the graph $G \times U$ defined by

$$(G \times U).V = G.V \times U.V,$$

and

$$\{(g, u), (h, v)\} \in (G \times U).E$$
$$\equiv$$
$$(\{g, h\} \in G.E \wedge u = v) \vee (g = h \wedge \{u, v\} \in U.E).$$

Elementary properties of $G \times U$ are $d(G \times U) = d(G) + d(U)$, $k(G \times U) = k(G) + k(U)$, $|(G \times U).E| = |G.E| \cdot |U.V| + |G.V| \cdot |U.E|$, and $\overline{k}(G \times U) = \overline{k}(G) + \overline{k}(U)$.

The *set of all functions from set A to set B* is denoted by B^A. An element b of B^A is sometimes denoted by $b(i : i \in A)$, where $\forall (i : i \in A : b(i) \in B)$.

Before introducing the braid operation we give an example to clarify the definition of braiding.

Example 3.1

Let G be the ring graph $R(4)$ and U be the complete graph $K(2)$. Consider the graph $G \times U^2$. Its edge set is given by

$$\{(g, (u(0), u(1))), (h, (v(0), v(1)))\} \in (G \times U^2).E$$
$$\equiv$$
$$\{g, h\} \in G.E \wedge u(0) = v(0) \wedge u(1) = v(1)$$
$$\vee$$
$$g = h \wedge \{u(0), v(0)\} \in U.E \wedge u(1) = v(1)$$
$$\vee$$
$$g = h \wedge u(0) = v(0) \wedge \{u(1), v(1)\} \in U.E$$

for all $g, h \in G.V$ and $u(0), u(1), v(0)$, and $v(1) \in U.V$. Informally one can say that two vertices share an edge if they are adjacent in exactly one index. Consequently, $G \times U^2$ has degree 4. A pictorial representation is given in figure 3.2.

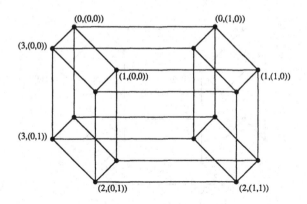

Figure 3.2: $R(4) \times K(2)^2$

Next we describe a subgraph B of this cartesian product graph in which the degree of each vertex is systematically reduced by 1.

$B.V = G.V \times (U.V)^2$, and

$\equiv$
$$\{(g, (u(0), u(1))), (h, (v(0), v(1)))\} \in B.E$$

$$\{g, h\} \in G.E \wedge u(0) = v(0) \wedge u(1) = v(1)$$
$\vee$
$$g = h \wedge \{u(0), v(0)\} \in U.E \ \wedge u(1) = v(1) \wedge g \bmod 2 = 0$$
$\vee$
$$g = h \wedge u(0) = v(0) \wedge \{u(1), v(1)\} \in U.E \wedge g \bmod 2 = 1$$

for all $g, h \in G.V$ and $u(0), u(1), v(0),$ and $v(1) \in U.V$. This graph is depicted in figure 3.3.

In fact, we have defined a function α from $G.V$ to $\{0, 1\}$ such that

$\equiv$
$$\{(g, u), (h, v)\} \in B.E$$

$$\{g, h\} \in G.E \wedge u = v$$
$\vee$
$$g = h \wedge \forall(i : i \in \{0, 1\} \wedge i \neq \alpha(g) : u(i) = v(i)) \wedge \{u(\alpha(g)), v(\alpha(g))\} \in U.E,$$

for all $g, h \in G.V$ and $u, v \in (U.V)^{\{0,1\}}$.
(End of example)

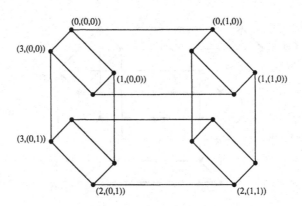

Figure 3.3: $b(R(4), K(2), \alpha)$

The braid operation is now introduced. The *braid* of two graphs, G and U, and a function α from $G.V$ to a finite set A, is the graph $b(G, U, \alpha)$ with

$$b(G, U, \alpha).V = G.V \times (U.V)^A$$

and for all $g, h \in G.V$ and $u, v \in (U.V)^A$

$$
\begin{aligned}
&\{(g, u), (h, v)\} \in b(G, U, \alpha).E \\
\equiv\ &\\
&\{g, h\} \in G.E \wedge u = v \\
&\vee \\
&g = h \wedge \forall (i : i \in A \wedge i \neq \alpha(g) : u(i) = v(i)) \wedge \{u(\alpha(g)), v(\alpha(g))\} \in U.E .
\end{aligned}
$$

Note 3.4
Since $b(G, U, \alpha)$ is a subgraph of the cartesian product graph $G \times U^{|A|}$, it is indeed a graph in the sense that it has neither multiple edges between two vertices nor self-loops, i.e., edges from a vertex to itself.
The graph $b(G, U, \alpha)$ is not necessarily connected (see example 3.8).
(End of note)

Property 3.5
For all graphs G and U, and each function $\alpha : G.V \to A$, where $|A| = 1$, we have
    $b(G, U, \alpha) = G \times U$.
In particular, if $|G.V| = 1$, then
    $b(G, U, \alpha) = U$.
(End of property)

Property 3.6
For all graphs G and U, and each function $\alpha : G.V \to A$, such that $|U.V| = 1$, we have

$b(G, U, \alpha) = G.$

(End of property)

Properties 3.5 and 3.6 express the fact that the cartesian product operation is a special braid operation, and that each graph is a braid graph.

Proposition 3.7
For all graphs G and U, and each function $\alpha : G.V \to A$ we have

(i) $|b(G, U, \alpha).V| = |G.V| \cdot |U.V|^{|A|}$,

(ii) $d(b(G, U, \alpha)) = d(G) + d(U)$, and

(iii) $|b(G, U, \alpha).E| = (|G.E| \cdot |U.V| + |G.V| \cdot |U.E|) \cdot |U.V|^{|A|-1}$.

Proof

(i)   is clear.

(ii) From $d((g, u)) = d_G(g) + d_U(u(\alpha(g)))$, for all $g \in G.V$ and $u \in (U.V)^A$, where $d_G(g)$ and $d_U(u)$ denote the degree of a vertex in G and U, respectively the assertion follows.

(iii) $2 \cdot |b(G, U, \alpha).E|$
$=$ { property 2.3 and $d((g, u)) = d_G(g) + d_U(u(\alpha(g)))$ }
        $S(g, u : (g, u) \in b(G, U, \alpha).V : d_G(g) + d_U(u(\alpha(g))))$
$=$ { def. of braiding, calculus }
        $S(u : u \in (U.V)^A : S(g : g \in G.V : d_G(g)))$
        $+ S(g : g \in G.V : S(u : u \in (U.V)^A : d_U(u(\alpha(g)))))$
$=$ { property 2.3, calculus }
        $2 \cdot |G.E| \cdot |U.V|^{|A|} + S(g : g \in G.V : 2 \cdot |U.V|^{|A|-1} \cdot |U.E|)$
$=$ { calculus }
        $2 \cdot (|G.E| \cdot |U.V| + |G.V| \cdot |U.E|) \cdot |U.V|^{|A|-1}$.

(End of proof and proposition)

From proposition 3.7(ii), note 3.4 and the properties of the cartesian product operation we conclude that $b(G, U, \alpha)$ is a subgraph of $G \times U^{|A|}$ in which the degree of a vertex, and, hence, the total number of edges, is strongly reduced. We end this section with an example.

Example 3.8
Let G be the ring graph $R(4)$, and U be the complete graph $K(2)$(see chapter 1). Define the function β from $G.V$ to $\{0,1\}$ by $\beta(g) = 0$. The resulting braid graph $b(G, U, \beta)$ is shown in figure 3.9.

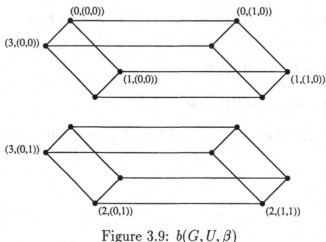

Figure 3.9: $b(G, U, \beta)$

This example shows that the braid of two connected graphs is not necessarily connected. In the next section we will formulate necessary and sufficient conditions for braid graphs to be connected.
(End of example)

3.2 The distance between two vertices in a braid graph

From example 3.8 we conclude that a braid graph is not necessarily connected. In order to handle disconnected graphs we define the distance between two vertices not joined by a path to be infinite. In this section we give a formula for the distance between two vertices, derive from it the diameter of a braid graph, and describe a routing algorithm.

Let (g, u) and (h, v) be two vertices of $b(G, U, \alpha)$, and consider a shortest path from (g, u) to (h, v). Such a path consists of two parts. One part corresponds to a path in

G from g to h, the other part is a collection of paths in $b(G, U, \alpha)$, each corresponding to a path in U from $u(a)$ to $v(a)$ for some a in $\{i : i \in A \wedge u(i) \neq v(i) : i\}$.

We first consider the G-part of the path from (g, u) to (h, v). Suppose $u(a) \neq v(a)$, for $a \in A$. An edge $\{(l, x), (m, y)\}$ of $b(G, U, \alpha)$ with $x(a) \neq y(a)$ satisfies $l = m \wedge \alpha(l) = a$. Hence each path from (g, u) to (h, v) has to visit a vertex (l, x) of $b(G, U, \alpha)$ for which $\alpha(l) = a$ holds. This observation leads to the following definition.

For all g, h and I, such that $g, h \in G.V \wedge I \subseteq A$, the *travelling length* $t_0(g, h, I)$ is defined as the length of a shortest path $p(j : 0 \leq j \leq n)$ in G satisfying

$$p(0) = g \wedge p(n) = h \wedge I \subseteq \{j : 0 \leq j \leq n : \alpha(p(j))\} \ .$$

(If such a path does not exist, we take $t_0(g, h, I) = \infty$).

Next we give two properties of travelling lengths. The first property states that, when $I = \{\}$, then the travelling length between two vertices equals their distance in graph G, and that the travelling length preserves monoticity of sets.

Property 3.10
For all g, h, I, and J, such that $g, h \in G.V \wedge I \subseteq J \subseteq A$, we have

(i) $t_0(g, h, \{\}) = k_G(g, h)$ and

(ii) $t_0(g, h, I) \leq t_0(g, h, J)$,

where $\{\}$ denotes the empty set and $k_G(g, h)$ denotes the distance between g and h in graph G.
(End of property)

Property 3.11
For all g, h, l, and I, such that $g, h, l \in G.V \wedge \{h, l\} \in G.E \wedge I \subseteq A$, we have

$$t_0(g, h, I) \leq t_0(g, l, I) + 1 \ .$$

(End of property)

Next we consider the U-part of a path in $b(G, U, \alpha)$. For all u and v, with $u, v \in (U.V)^A$, we define the *difference set* $D(u, v)$ by

$$D(u, v) = \{i : i \in A \wedge u(i) \neq v(i) : i\},$$

and the *traversing length* $t_1(u, v)$ by

$$t_1(u, v) = \mathbf{S}(i : i \in A : k_U(u(i), v(i)))$$

where, for $i \in A$, $k_U(u(i), v(i))$ denotes the distance between $u(i)$ and $v(i)$ in graph U. Notice that $t_1(u, v)$ is the distance between u and v in the cartesian product graph $U^{|A|}$.

Property 3.12
For all u and v, such that $u, v \in (U.V)^A \wedge u \neq v$, we have

$$0 = t_1(u, u) < t_1(u, v) \leq |D(u, v)| \cdot k_U \leq |A| \cdot k_U ,$$

where k_U denotes the diameter of graph U.
(End of property)

Property 3.13
For all $i, u, v,$ and x, such that $i \in A \wedge u, v, x \in (U.V)^A \wedge \{v(i), x(i)\} \in U.E \wedge \forall(j : j \in A \wedge j \neq i : v(j) = x(j))$, we have

$$t_1(u, v) \leq t_1(u, x) + 1 .$$

(End of property)

Equipped with these definitions and properties we can prove

Theorem 3.14
For all $g, h, u,$ and v, such that $(g, u), (h, v) \in G.V \times (U.V)^A$, we have

$$k((g, u), (h, v)) = t_0(g, h, D(u, v)) + t_1(u, v) .$$

Proof
Define $\delta : b(G, U, \alpha).V \times b(G, U, \alpha).V \rightarrow \mathbb{N} \cup \{\infty\}$ by

$$\delta((g, u), (h, v)) = t_0(g, h, D(u, v)) + t_1(u, v) .$$

Then δ satisfies the following properties.

(0) $\delta((g, u), (h, v)) = 0 \equiv g = h \wedge u = v$,
(1) $\{(h, v), (l, x)\} \in b(G, U, \alpha).E \Rightarrow \delta((g, u), (h, v)) \leq \delta((g, u), (l, x)) + 1 ,$
(2) $\quad 0 < \delta((g, u), (h, v)) < \infty \quad \Rightarrow$
     $\exists(l, x : \{(h, v), (l, x)\} \in b(G, U, \alpha).E : \delta((g, u), (h, v)) \geq \delta((g, u), (l, x)) + 1).$

Properties (0) and (1) follow immediately from properties 3.10-3.13. Next we prove (2).

$$0 < \delta((g, u), (h, v)) < \infty$$
$\Rightarrow$ { def. of δ, calculus }
$$0 < t_0(g, h, D(u, v)) + t_1(u, v) < \infty \ \wedge \ \alpha(h) \in D(u, v)$$
$\vee$
$$0 < t_0(g, h, D(u, v)) + t_1(u, v) < \infty \ \wedge \ \alpha(h) \notin D(u, v)$$
$\Rightarrow$ { property 3.12, property 3.10 }
$$0 < t_1(u, v) < \infty \ \wedge \ \alpha(h) \in D(u, v)$$
$\vee$
$$0 < t_0(g, h, D(u, v)) < \infty \ \wedge \ \alpha(h) \notin D(u, v)$$
$\Rightarrow$ { calculus }
$$\exists(x : \{(h, v), (h, x)\} \in b(G, U, \alpha).E :$$
$$D(u, x) \subseteq D(u, v) \wedge t_1(u, x) + 1 = t_1(u, v))$$
$\vee$
$$\exists(l : \{(h, v), (l, v)\} \in b(G, U, \alpha).E :$$
$$t_0(g, l, D(u, v)) + 1 = t_0(g, h, D(u, v)))$$
$\Rightarrow$ { property 3.10 }
$$\exists(x : \{(h, v), (h, x)\} \in b(G, U, \alpha).E :$$
$$t_0(g, h, D(u, x)) + t_1(u, x) + 1 \leq t_0(g, h, D(u, v)) + t_1(u, v))$$
$\vee$
$$\exists(l : \{(h, v), (l, v)\} \in b(G, U, \alpha).E :$$
$$t_0(g, l, D(u, v)) + t_1(u, v) + 1 \leq t_0(g, h, D(u, v)) + t_1(u, v))$$
$\Rightarrow$ { calculus, def. of δ }
$$\exists(l, x : \{(h, v), (l, x)\} \in b(G, U, \alpha).E :$$
$$\delta((g, u), (l, x)) + 1 \leq \delta((g, u), (h, v))) .$$

Hence, on acount of the property of the diameter stated in Chapter 1, $k = \delta$. (End of proof and theorem)

From theorem 3.14 we deduce several consequences. A first consequence concerns the diameter k of $b(G, U, \alpha)$.

Corollary 3.15

If $|U.V| > 1$ then we have

$$k = \mathbf{MAX}(g, h : g, h \in G.V : t_0(g, h, A)) + |A| \cdot k_U \ .$$

Proof

$$k$$

$=$ { theorem 3.14 }

$\mathbf{MAX}(g, h, u, v : (g, u), (h, v) \in b(G, U, \alpha).V : t_0(g, h, D(u, v)) + t_1(u, v))$

$=$ { take u and v such that $\forall(i : i \in A : k_U(u(i), v(i)) = k_U)$,

$\quad\quad |U.V| > 1 \Rightarrow D(u, v) = A$, property 3.10, and property 3.12 }

$\mathbf{MAX}(g, h : g, h \in G.V : t_0(g, h, A) + |A| \cdot k_U)$

$=$ { calculus }

$\mathbf{MAX}(g, h : g, h \in G.V : t_0(g, h, A)) + |A| \cdot k_U \ .$

(End of proof and corollary)

From corollary 3.15 we derive necessary and sufficient conditions for a braid graph to be connected.

Corollary 3.16

For all graphs G and U, and each function $\alpha : G.V \to A$, such that $|U.V| > 1$, we have

$$b(G, U, \alpha) \text{ is connected } \equiv G \text{ and } U \text{ are connected and } \alpha \text{ is surjective.}$$

Proof

$\quad b(G, U, \alpha)$ is connected

$=$ { def. of connectedness }

$\quad k < \infty$

$=$ { corollary 3.15, calculus }

$\quad \forall(g, h : g, h \in G.V : t_0(g, h, A) < \infty) \wedge k_U < \infty$

$=$ { def. of t_0 and connectedness }

$\quad G$ is connected $\wedge \alpha$ is surjective $\wedge U$ is connected.

(End of proof and corollary)

According to property 3.6 we have for all graphs G and U, and each function $\alpha :$ $G.V \rightarrow A$, such that $|U.V| = 1$,

$$b(G, U, \alpha) \text{ is connected } \equiv G \text{ is connected.}$$

We conclude this section with a shortest path routing algorithm for a connected braid graph.

Let $b(G, U, \alpha)$ be connected, and let shp_in_U denote a shortest path routing algorithm in U. We use the following specification for shp_in_U within $b(G, U, \alpha)$.

$\{z = (l, x) \land w \in U.V\}$
$shp\_in\_U(x(\alpha(l)), w)$
$\{z = (l, y) \land \forall(i : i \in A \land i \neq \alpha(l) : y(i) = x(i)) \land y(\alpha(l)) = w\}.$

Informally, for a vertex (l, x) of $b(G, U, \alpha)$ and an element w of $U.V$, a path from the $\alpha(l)$-th index of x to w is established by $shp\_in\_U(x(\alpha(l)), w)$ without affecting any other index of x or l.

Furthermore, we assume that for all g, h, and I, with $g, h \in G.V \land I \subseteq A$, a shortest path $q(j : 0 \leq j \leq n)$ in G can be determined such that $q(0) = g \land q(n) = h \land I \subseteq \{j : 0 \leq j \leq n : \alpha(q(j))\}.$

Let (g, u) and (h, v) be two vertices of $b(G, U, \alpha)$ and let $p(i : 0 \leq i \leq n)$ be a shortest path in G satisfying $p(0) = g \land p(n) = h \land D(u, v) \subseteq \{i : 0 \leq i \leq n : \alpha(p(i))\}$. Then the algorithm reads

```
    i := 0;  (l, x) := (g, u)   {(l, x) = (g, u)}
;   do i < n → shp_in_U(x(α(l)), v(α(l)))
            ;   (l, x) := (p(i + 1), x)
            ;   i := i + 1
    od
;   shp_in_U(x(α(l)), v(α(l)))
    {(l, x) = (h, v)}
```

where i is an integer, and l and x are variables from $G.V$ and $(U.V)^A$, respectively.

The correctness of the algorithm can be verified by choosing

$$k((g, u), (l, x)) + k((l, x), (h, v)) = k((g, u), (h, v))$$

as an invariant of its loop.

Obviously, the main difficulty is to determine such paths $p(g, h, D(u, v))$. For instance, for an arbitrary graph G, for α the identity function from $G.V$ to $G.V$, and $g \in G.V$, determining $t_0(g, g, G.V)$ reduces to the problem "does G contain a Hamiltonian cycle, i.e., a path in G with the same initial and terminal vertex which visits each other vertex exactly once". A problem that is known to be NP-complete (see [Even79]). As we have argued in Chapter 2 our interest is in graphs with a regular interconnection pattern. The consequences of this restriction are investigated in the next section.

3.3 Vertex-transitive braid graphs

In the preceding sections and chapters we have often used the phrase "a graph with a regular interconnection pattern" without explicitly stating its meaning. The problem is that no appropriate definition for the notion "regularly connected" can be given. In case of processor networks the tendency, however, is to translate regularly connected by vertex-transitive. The property that in a vertex-transitive graph each vertex has the same view of the graph makes vertex-transitive graphs attractive candidates for processor networks. Several systems proposed as processor networks are indeed vertex-transitive. Meshes, cube-connected cycles, and k-ary n-cubes are well-known examples of such systems.

In recent works([Aker86, Anne87]) it has been shown that vertex-transitive graphs are graphs whose interconnection pattern is governed by a group. This result admits the possibility of deriving properties of vertex-transitive graphs by applying group theory. A drawback, however, is that given a vertex-transitive graph it is not easy to find the group governing the interconnection pattern of the graph.

We start with some definitions. Two vertices x and y of a graph G are said to be adjacent if $\{x, y\} \in G.E$. An *automorphism of a graph* is a permutation of its vertices that preserves adjacency. An automorphism f of graph G thus satisfies

- f is a one-to-one mapping from $G.V$ to $G.V$, and

- $\forall(x, y : x, y \in G.V : \{x, y\} \in G.E \equiv \{f(x), f(y)\} \in G.E)$.

A graph is defined to be *vertex-transitive* if for any two vertices x and y there exists an automorphism of the graph that maps x to y.

Since an automorphism maps a path of length n onto a path of length n, we have

Property 3.17
For all graphs G we have

$$G \text{ is vertex-transitive } \Rightarrow G \text{ is distance-regular.}$$

(End of property)

Vertex-transitivity and distance-regularity are not equivalent notions.

Example 3.18
Consider the graph G depicted in figure 3.19.

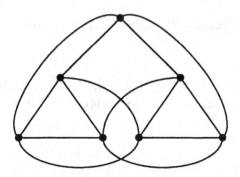

Figure 3.19: A distance-regular graph

Straight calculation shows that each vertex has one vertex at distance 0, four vertices at distance 1, and two vertices at distance 2. Hence, G is distance-regular. G is not vertex-transitive, because the vertices at distance 2 are adjacent for only four vertices. We may also say that a distance-regular graph does not necessarily have the property that the graph looks the same from each of its vertices. We therefore restrict our attention to vertex-transitive graphs.
(End of example)

We proceed by investigating under what conditions braiding preserves vertex-transitivity. First we notice that vertex-transitivity of both G and U is not sufficient to guarantee that $b(G, U, \alpha)$ be vertex-transitive.

Example 3.20

Let G be the graph $R(3)$, and let U be the graph $K(2)$. Ring graphs and complete graphs are trivial examples of vertex-transitive graphs, so both G and U are vertex-transitive. Define the function α from $G.V$ onto $\{0,1\}$ by $\alpha(g) = g \bmod 2$. The braid graph $b(G, U, \alpha)$ is shown in figure 3.21.

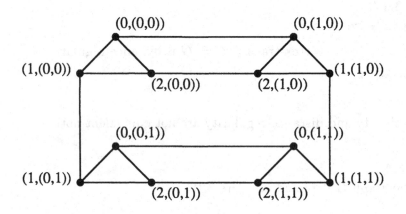

Figure 3.21: $b(R(3), K(2), g \bmod 2)$

Vertex $(0, (0,0))$ is in the 4-cycle $(0, (0,0))$, $(2, (0,0))$, $(2, (1,0))$, $(0, (1,0))$, $(0, (0,0))$, but vertex $(1, (0,0))$ is not in any 4-cycle, so $b(G, U, \alpha)$ is not vertex-transitive. (End of example)

Example 3.20 suggests that the elements of $G.V$ have to be homogeneously distributed over A by α. For that purpose we introduce an equivalence relation on $G.V$. The *equivalence relation on $G.V$ induced by α*, denoted by $\sim_\alpha$, is the relation defined by

$$g \sim_\alpha h \equiv \alpha(g) = \alpha(h) ,$$

for all $g, h \in G.V$. For $g \in G.V$, the equivalence class to which g belongs is denoted by $[g]_\alpha$. When α is obvious from the context, the subscript is omitted.

In example 3.20 we have $\|[0]\| = 2 > 1 = \|[1]\|$, so not all equivalence classes have the same number of elements. Even if all equivalence classes have the same number of elements and G and U are vertex-transitive, then $b(G, U, \alpha)$ is not necessarily vertex-transitive.

Example 3.22
Let G be the graph $R(6)$, and U be the graph $K(2)$. Define α from $G.V$ onto $\{0, 1, 2\}$ by $\alpha(0) = \alpha(5) = 0$, $\alpha(1) = \alpha(3) = 1$, and $\alpha(2) = \alpha(4) = 2$. The vertex $(0, (0, 0, 0))$ is in the 4-cycle $(0, (0, 0, 0)), (5, (0, 0, 0)), (5, (1, 0, 0)), (0, (1, 0, 0)), (0, (0, 0, 0))$. Using some case analysis one can show that $(1, (0, 0, 0))$ is not in a 4-cycle.
(End of example)

Define for $g \in G.V$, the subgraph of G induced on $[g]$, denoted as $G_{[g]}$, by

$$\begin{aligned} G_{[g]}.V &= [g] \text{ , and for all } h, l \in [g] \\ \{h, l\} \in G_{[g]}.E &\equiv \{h, l\} \in G.E \text{ .} \end{aligned}$$

Example 3.22 reveals that some correspondence between the subgraphs induced on the equivalence classes is necessary. In the following definitions a correspondence is described.

An α-*automorphism* of a graph G is an automorphism f of G that preserves the equivalence relation induced by α, i.e., f satisfies

$$\forall(g, h : g, h \in G.V : g \in [h] \equiv f(g) \in [f(h)]) \text{ .}$$

G is α-*vertex-transitive* if for any two vertices g and h of G an α-automorphism exists that maps g onto h.

Notice that, when G is α-vertex-transitive, any two equivalence classes have the same number of elements. When α is an injective function, the equivalence relation induced by α is the identity relation. Hence,

Property 3.23
For all graphs G and each injective function $\alpha : G.V \to A$ we have

$$G \text{ is vertex-transitive} \equiv G \text{ is } \alpha\text{-vertex-transitive .}$$

(end of property)

The next example shows that the injectivity of α is not a necessary condition to achieve G's being α-vertex-transitive.

Example 3.24

Let G be a starred polygon(see Chapter 1) with n vertices. G is vertex-transitive, because the function $f : G.V \to G.V$ defined by $f(v(i)) = v((i+1) \bmod n)$ is an automorphism of G. Let s be a divisor of n and consider the mapping α from $G.V$ to $A = \{i : 0 \leq i < s : i\}$ defined by $\alpha(v(i)) = i \bmod s$. From

$$v(i) \in [v(j)]$$
$$= \quad \{ \text{ def. of } [\,] \text{ and } \alpha \}$$
$$i \bmod s = j \bmod s$$
$$= \quad \{ \text{ s divides n } \}$$
$$((i+1) \bmod n) \bmod s = ((j+1) \bmod n) \bmod s$$
$$= \quad \{ \text{ def. of } f \text{ and } \alpha \}$$
$$\alpha(f(v(i))) = \alpha(f(v(j)))$$
$$= \quad \{ \text{ def. of } [\,] \}$$
$$f(v(i)) \in [f(v(j))]$$

we conclude that f is also an α-automorphism of G. Hence, G is α-vertex-transitive.

Consequently, graph G in example 3.1 is α-vertex-transitive. By considering the function β in the example 3.8, defined as $\beta(g) = g \bmod 1$, we see that G is also β-vertex-transitive.

(End of example)

Let G and H be graphs, and α and β be functions from $G.V$ to a set A and from $H.V$ to a set B, respectively. We define the function $\alpha \times \beta$ from $G.V \times H.V$ to $A \times B$ by

$$(\alpha \times \beta)(g, h) = (\alpha(g), \beta(h)) .$$

The equivalence relation on $G.V \times H.V$ induced by $(\alpha \times \beta)$ is the relation $\sim_{\alpha \times \beta}$ defined by

$$(g, h) \sim_{\alpha \times \beta} (l, m) \equiv g \sim_\alpha l \wedge h \sim_\beta m ,$$

where $g, l \in G.V$ and $h, m \in H.V$. The product of an α-automorphism of G and a β-automorphism of H is an $(\alpha \times \beta)$-automorphism of $G \times H$. Thus we have

Property 3.25
For all graphs G and H, and functions $\alpha : G.V \to A$ and $\beta : H.V \to B$ we have

$\qquad$ G is α-vertex-transitive and H is β-vertex-transitive

$\Rightarrow$

$\qquad$ $G \times H$ is $(\alpha \times \beta)$-vertex-transitive .

(End of property)

Properties 3.23 and 3.25 and example 3.24 demonstrate that the notion "α-vertex-transitive" is not too restrictive. It derives its right of existence from the following theorem.

Theorem 3.26
For all graphs G and U, and each function $\alpha : G.V \to A$ we have

$\qquad$ G is α-vertex-transitive $\wedge$ U is vertex-transitive

$\Rightarrow$

$\qquad$ $b(G, U, \alpha)$ is vertex-transitive .

Proof
For each pair of vertices x and y of $b(G, U, \alpha)$ we have to exhibit a one-to-one mapping $M : b(G, U, \alpha).V \to b(G, U, \alpha).V$ satisfying

(i) $\forall (w, z :: \{w, z\} \in b(G, U, \alpha).E \equiv \{M(w), M(z)\} \in b(G, U, \alpha).E)$,

(ii) $M(x) = y$.

First we observe that each α-automorphism f of G induces a function $\underline{f}$ from A to A defined by

$$\underline{f}(i) = \textbf{if } i \in \alpha(G.V) \to \alpha(f(g))$$
$$\quad [\![\ i \notin \alpha(G.V) \to i$$
$$\textbf{fi} \ ,$$

where $g \in G.V$ satisfies $\alpha(g) = i$. This definition is sound, for $\alpha(g) = \alpha(h) \equiv \alpha(f(g)) = \alpha(f(h))$. Notice that $\underline{f}(\alpha(g)) = \alpha(f(g))$ holds. Second, by using the same equivalence we deduce that $\underline{f}$ is injective. Since A is a finite set, it follows that $\underline{f}$ is a permutation.

This observation leads us to the following definition of the function M_f from $b(G, U, \alpha)$ to itself:

$$M_f((g, u)) = (f(g), u') \,,$$

where $\forall(i : i \in A : u'(\underline{f}(i)) = u(i))$.

From

$\quad M_f((g, u)) = M_f((h, v))$
$=\qquad\{$ def. of M_f $\}$
$\quad (f(g), u') = (f(h), v')$
$=\qquad\{$ calculus $\}$
$\quad f(g) = f(h) \land \forall(i : i \in A : u'(i) = v'(i))$
$=\qquad\{$ f is an automorphism of G, $\underline{f}$ is a permutation of A $\}$
$\quad g = h \land \forall(i : i \in A : u'(\underline{f}(i)) = v'(\underline{f}(i)))$
$=\qquad\{$ def. of M_f $\}$
$\quad g = h \land \forall(i : i \in A : u(i) = v(i))$

we conclude that $(g, u) = (h, v) \equiv M_f((g, u)) = M_f((h, v))$, so M_f is injective, and, due to the finiteness of $b(G, U, \alpha)$, M_f is bijective.

Consequently, in order to prove that M_f is an automorphism of $b(G, U, \alpha)$, it remains to demonstrate that M_f preserves adjacency.

For $(g, u), (h, v) \in b(G, U, \alpha).V$ we have

$\quad \{(g, u), (h, v)\} \in b(G, U, \alpha).E \land g = h$
$=\qquad\{$ def. of braiding $\}$
$\quad g = h \land \forall(i : i \in A \land i \neq \alpha(g) : u(i) = v(i)) \land \{u(\alpha(g)), v(\alpha(g))\} \in U.E$
$=\qquad\{$ u', v' as in the def. of M_f, f is an automorphism of G $\}$
$\quad f(g) = f(h) \land \forall(j : j \in A \land j \neq \underline{f}(\alpha(g)) : u'(j) = v'(j))$
$\qquad\qquad \land\{u'(\underline{f}(\alpha(g))), v'(\underline{f}(\alpha(g)))\} \in U.E$
$=\qquad\{$ $\underline{f}(\alpha(g)) = \alpha(f(g))$ $\}$
$\quad f(g) = f(h) \land \forall(j : j \in A \land j \neq \alpha(f(g)) : u'(j) = v'(j))$
$\qquad\qquad \land\{u'(\alpha(f(g))), v'(\alpha(f(g)))\} \in U.E$
$=\qquad\{$ def. of $b(G, U, \alpha).E$ $\}$
$\quad \{M_f((g, u)), M_f((h, v))\} \in b(G, U, \alpha).E \land f(g) = f(h)$
and

$$\{(g,u),(h,v)\} \in b(G,U,\alpha).E \wedge g \neq h$$
$$= \quad \{ \text{ def. of } b(G,U,\alpha).E \}$$
$$\{g,h\} \in G.E \wedge \forall(i : i \in A : u(i) = v(i))$$
$$= \quad \{ f \text{ is an automorphism of } G, \text{ def. of } M_f \}$$
$$\{f(g),f(h)\} \in G.E \wedge \forall(i : i \in A : u'(\underline{f}(i)) = v'(\underline{f}(i)))$$
$$= \quad \{ \underline{f} \text{ is a permutation on } A \}$$
$$\{f(g),f(h)\} \in G.E \wedge u' = v'$$
$$= \quad \{ \text{ def. of } b(G,U,\alpha).E, \text{ def. of } M_f \}$$
$$\{M_f((g,u)), M_f((h,v))\} \in b(G,U,\alpha).E \wedge f(g) \neq f(h) .$$

Thus M_f is an automorphism of $b(G,U,\alpha).E$.

Let $\Gamma(U)$ be the set of automorphisms of graph U. For $c \in \Gamma(U)^A$ we define the function $P_c : b(G,U,\alpha).V \to b(G,U,\alpha).V$ by

$$P_c((g,u)) = (g,c(u)) ,$$

where $\forall(i : i \in A : (c(u))(i) = c(i)(u(i)))$. Using the definitions of $b(G,U,\alpha).E$ and P_c one proves that P_c is an automorphism of $b(G,U,\alpha)$.

Equipped with these automorphisms M_f and P_c we can exhibit the required mapping M. Let $x = (g,u)$ and $y = (h,v)$. Since G is α-vertex-transitive, an α-automorphism f of G exists that maps g onto h. Thus $M_f((g,u)) = (h,u')$ with $\forall(i : i \in A : u'(\underline{f}(i)) = u(i))$. Since U is vertex-transitive an element c of $\Gamma(U)^A$ exists with $c(u') = v$. Hence $M = P_c \circ M_f$ is an automorphism of $b(G,U,\alpha)$ mapping x onto y. (End of proof and theorem)

Corollary 3.27
For all graphs G and U, and each function $\alpha : G.V \to A$, such that G is α-vertex-transitive and connected, U is vertex-transitive and connected, and α is surjective, we have

$$b(G,U,\alpha) \text{ is vertex-transitive and connected} \wedge |A| \text{ is a divisor of } |G.V| .$$

Proof
The validity of the first conjunct follows from theorem 3.26 and corollary 3.16. To prove the second conjunct, we observe that from G is α-vertex-transitive it follows that all equivalence classes have the same number of elements, and that the surjectivity of α implies that $|A|$ is the number of distinct equivalence classes. (End of proof and corollary)

Intermezzo 3.28

We could also define another braid operation. Let G and U be graphs, and τ be a function from a finite set A to $G.V$. The graph $ab(G, U, \tau)$ is the graph H with

$$H.V = G.V \times (U.V)^A$$

and for all $g, h \in G.V$ and $u, v \in (U.V)^A$

$$
\equiv
\begin{array}{l}
\{(g, u), (h, v)\} \in H.E \\[6pt]
\{g, h\} \in G.E \wedge u = v \\
\vee \\
\quad g = h \wedge \mathbf{N}(i : i \in A : u(i) \neq v(i)) = 1 \;\; \wedge \\
\quad \forall(i : i \in A \wedge u(i) \neq v(i) : g = \tau(i) \wedge \{u(i), v(i)\} \in U.E) \, .
\end{array}
$$

Using similar arguments and definitions one can prove that, to obtain connected, vertex-transitive graphs $ab(G, U, \tau)$, τ has to be surjective and every two equivalence classes in A have to be isomorphic. In that case we have that $|A|$ is a multiple of $|G.V|$ and all equivalence classes have $n = \frac{|A|}{|G.V|}$ elements. Rearranging the elements of A according to the equivalence relation $\sim_\tau$, one gets the graph H with

$$H.V = G.V \times (U.V^n)^{G.V}$$

and for all $g, h \in G.V$ and $u, v \in (U.V^n)^{G.V}$

$$
\equiv
\begin{array}{l}
\{(g, u), (h, v)\} \in H.E \\[6pt]
\{g, h\} \in G.E \wedge u = v \\
\vee \\
\quad g = h \wedge \mathbf{N}(j : j \in G.V : u(j) \neq v(j)) = 1 \;\; \wedge \\
\quad \forall(j : j \in G.V \wedge u(j) \neq v(j) : g = j \wedge \{u(j), v(j)\} \in U.E^n) \, .
\end{array}
$$

So the same graph could be obtained by applying the braid operation b on G and U^n with $\alpha = id$ and $A = G.V$.

(End of intermezzo)

We end this section with an example of a class of connected, vertex-transitive braid graphs.

Example 3.29
Let G be a starred polygon with Hamiltonian cycle $v(i : 0 \leq i \leq n)$, and let U be a connected, vertex-transitive graph. Let s be a divisor of n and α be the mapping from $G.V = \{i : 0 \leq i < n : v(i)\}$ to $A = \{i : 0 \leq i < s : i\}$ defined by $\alpha(v(i)) = i \bmod s$. According to example 3.24 graph G is α-vertex-transitive, and, hence, $b(G, U, \alpha)$ is vertex-transitive.

When we take for G the graph $R(n)$ we get an interesting class of braid graphs, which we will call the *graph-connected rings*. These graphs are the topic of the next section.

If we take for U and s a ring graph and 2, respectively, another interesting class of braid graphs appears. The members of this class are called the *torus-connected graphs* and are considered in section 3.5.
(End of example)

3.4 The graph-connected rings

In this section attention is restricted to one specific class of the braid graphs described in example 3.29. We take for G the ring graph $R(n)$, for U a connected, vertex-transitive graph, and consider the connected, vertex-transitive graph $b(G, U, \alpha)$ with $\alpha : R(n).V \rightarrow A = \{j : 0 \leq j < s : j\}$ defined by

$$\alpha(i) = i \bmod s,$$

where s is a divisor of n.

First we give its number of vertices and its degree, which are denoted by N and d, respectively.

$$N = n \cdot m^s \text{ , and}$$

$$d = \begin{cases} 1 + d_U, & \text{for } n = 2, \\ 2 + d_U, & \text{for } n > 2, \end{cases}$$

where m and d_U are the number of vertices of U and the degree of U, respectively. Notice that the degree of $b(G, U, \alpha)$ is independent of s, so by varying s a number of fixed degree graphs can be obtained.

Next an upper bound for the bisection width of $b(R(n), U, i \bmod s)$ in terms of the bisection widths of $B(R(n))$ and $B(U)$ is calculated. Note that $B(R(2)) = 1$ and $B(R(n)) = 2$ for $n > 2$. Since the best results are obtained for both n and m even, we restrict our attention to this case. In the analysis below we omit the domains of the bounded variables, viz. $g, h \in G.V$ and $u, v \in (U.V)^A$. Let $(S(G), T(G))$ and $(S(U), T(U))$ denote partitionings of $G.V$ and $U.V$ for which $B(G)$ and $B(U)$ are obtained, respectively. There are two obvious partitionings of $b(G, U, \alpha).V$.

The first one corresponds to the partitioning of $G.V$. We define S_0 and T_0 by

$$S_0 = \{g, u : g \in S(G) : (g, u)\} \text{ and}$$

$$T_0 = \{h, u : h \in T(G) : (h, u)\} \ .$$

Hence, we have

$$E(S_0.T_0) = \{g, h, u : \{g, h\} \in E(S(G), T(G)) : \{(g, u), (h, u\} \ \}$$

and

$$|E(S_0, T_0)| = \begin{cases} m^s, & \text{for } n = 2 \ , \\ 2 \cdot m^s, & \text{for } n > 2 \ . \end{cases}$$

The second partitioning corresponds to two collections, each consisting of $\frac{|U.V|^A}{2}$ copies of G. S_1 and T_1 are defined by

$$S_1 = \{g, u : u(0) \in S(U) : (g, u)\} \text{ and}$$

$$T_1 = \{g, v : v(0) \in T(U) : (g, v)\} \ .$$

Here we have

$$E(S_1, T_1) = \{g, u, v : g \bmod s = 0 \ \wedge \ \{u(0), v(0)\} \in E(S(U) , T(U)) : \\ \{(g, u), (g, v)\} \ \}$$

and

$$|E(S_1, T_1)| = \frac{n}{s} \cdot B(U) \cdot m^{s-1} \ .$$

Notice that because all equivalence classes have the same number of elements, the choice of $g \bmod s = 0$ is not relevant. Consequently,

Property 3.30

For the bisection width B of $b(R(n), U, i \bmod s)$ we have

$$B \leq \begin{cases} 2 \cdot m^s \ \mathbf{min} \ \frac{n}{s} \cdot B(U) \cdot m^{s-1}, & \text{for } n > 2 \,, \\ m^s \ \mathbf{min} \ \frac{n}{s} \cdot B(U) \cdot m^{s-1}, & \text{for } n = 2 \,, \end{cases}$$

where $m = |U.V|$, s/n, and n and m are even.
(End of property)

Although we cannot prove that these bounds are optimal, for our analysis we assume that equality holds. Under the assumption $B \cdot W = N$ we obtain for the width W of an edge of $b(G, U, \alpha)$:

Property 3.31

For the width W of a edge of $b(R(n), U, i \bmod s)$ we have

$$W = \begin{cases} \frac{n}{2} \ \mathbf{max} \ \frac{m \cdot s}{B(U)}, & \text{for } n > 2 \,, \\ 2 \ \mathbf{max} \ \frac{2 \cdot m}{B(U)}, & \text{for } n = 2 \,. \end{cases}$$

(End of property)

Hence by applying the braid operation graphs with wide edges can be obtained. The main reason for these wide edges is that the braid operation keeps the degree small with respect to the number of vertices. This nice property is absent in graphs obtained by applying the cartesian product operation.

Our next issue in the analysis of these graphs concerns the diameter. According to corollary 3.15 we have

$$k = s \cdot k_U + \mathbf{MAX}(g, h : 0 \leq g, h < n : t_0(g, h, A)) \,,$$

where $t_0(g, h, A)$ is the length of a shortest path $p(j : 0 \leq j \leq r)$ in $R(n)$ with $p(0) = g \wedge p(r) = h \wedge A \subseteq \{j : 0 \leq j \leq r : p(j) \bmod s\}$ and k_U denotes the diameter of U. Consider a pair of vertices, g and h say, such that $t_0(g, h, A)$ is maximal. Due to the α-vertex-transitivity of $R(n)$ we may choose g equal to 0. A path $p(j : 0 \leq j \leq r)$ with the above property can be considered as consisting of two parts. One part is a shortest A-complete path $p(j : 0 \leq j \leq r_0)$ starting in 0, i.e., $p(0) = 0$ and $A = \{j : 0 \leq j \leq r_0 : p(j) \bmod s\}$. The other part is a shortest path in $R(n)$ from $p(r_0)$ to h. Two such shortest A-complete paths exist. The first one corresponds to traversing the ring in a "clockwise direction":

$$p(i) = i \,, \text{ for } 0 \leq i \leq s - 1 \,.$$

Traversing the ring in the opposite direction gives the second A-complete path of length $(s-1)$:

$$p(i) = (n-i) \bmod n \ , \text{ for } 0 \le i \le s-1 \ .$$

Hence either $r_0 = s - 1$ or $r_0 = n - (s-1)$ holds, and we may rewrite the formula for k as

$$k = s \cdot k_U + s - 1 + \mathbf{MAX}(h : 0 \le h < n : k_G(s-1,h) \ \mathbf{min} \ k_G(n-(s-1),h))$$

where $k_G(x,y)$ denotes the distance between vertices x and y in G. In particular, if $s = 1$ we obtain the well-known formula for the diameter of the cartesian product graph $G \times U : k = k_G + k_U$.

The exact value of k depends on s.

Theorem 3.32

For the diameter k of $b(R(n), U, i \bmod s)$ we have

$$k = \begin{cases} n \ \mathbf{div} \ 2 + s \cdot k_U, & \text{for } 1 \le s \le n \ \mathbf{div} \ 4 + 1 \ , \\ 2 \cdot (s-1) + s \cdot k_U, & \text{for } n \ \mathbf{div} \ 4 + 1 < s \le n \ \mathbf{div} \ 2 \ \wedge \ n \ge 4 \ , \\ s + s \cdot k_U, & \text{for } 2 \le n \le 3 \ , \\ n - 2 + n \ \mathbf{div} \ 2 + n \cdot k_U, & \text{for } s = n \wedge n \ge 4 \ . \end{cases}$$

Proof

– For $1 \le s \le n \ \mathbf{div} \ 4 + 1$ we have

$$0 \le s - 1 \le n \ \mathbf{div} \ 4 \wedge n - n \ \mathbf{div} \ 4 \le n - (s-1) \le n \ ,$$

and, hence, for $0 \le h < n$, we derive

$$k_G(s-1,h) \ \mathbf{min} \ k_G(n-(s-1),h) \ \le \ k_G(s-1, n \ \mathbf{div} \ 2)$$
$$= \ n \ \mathbf{div} \ 2 - (s-1).$$

We thus find for the diameter $k = n \ \mathbf{div} \ 2 + s \cdot k_U$.

– In the same way as above we find, for $n \ \mathbf{div} \ 4 + 1 < s \le n \ \mathbf{div} \ 2 \ \wedge \ n \ge 4$, and for $0 \le h < n$,

$$k_G(s-1,h) \ \mathbf{min} \ k_G(n-(s-1),h) \le k_G(s-1,0) = s - 1 \ , \text{ and, so,}$$

$$k = 2 \cdot (s-1) + s \cdot k_U \ .$$

- If $2 \le n \le 3$ then we have

  $\mathbf{MAX}(h : 0 \le h < n : k_G(s-1, h) \; \mathbf{min} \; k_G(n - (s-1), h)) = 1$, and, hence,

  $k = s + s \cdot k_U$.

- For $s = n \wedge n \ge 4$ we have

  $\mathbf{MAX}(h : 0 \le h < n : k_G(n-1, h) \; \mathbf{min} \; k_G(1, h)) = n \; \mathbf{div} \; 2 - 1$.

  Hence, we obtain $\quad k = n - 2 + n \; \mathbf{div} \; 2 + n \cdot k_U$.

(End of proof and theorem)

From these formulae for the diameter we conclude that with the braid operation large, vertex-transitive graphs with a small degree and a small diameter can be constructed. In particular, if we choose $s = n$ and $U = K(m)$ we obtain interesting graphs that deserve special attention. Notice first that if $s = n$ the function α becomes the identity function. The graphs $b(R(n), K(m), id)$, proposed in a different setting by W.H. Hesselink and M.T. Kosters ([Hess86]), actually formed the starting point of the braid operation. The graph $b(R(n), K(m), id)$ has, for $n \ge 4$,

$$d = m + 1 \text{ and } k = 2n - 2 + n \; \mathbf{div} \; 2 ,$$

and, as we have proved,

$$W = \frac{n}{2} \; \mathbf{max} \; \frac{m \cdot n}{B(K(m))} .$$

Since $B(K(m)) = (\frac{m}{2})^2$, we thus find

$$W = \frac{n}{2} \; \mathbf{max} \; \frac{4 \cdot n}{m} ,$$

under the assumption $B \cdot W = n \cdot m^n$. It should further be noted that the same graphs also appear in [Anne87]. However in [Anne87] neither the degree, the diameter, the bisection width, nor a routing algorithm is presented. Since for $m = 2$ these graphs are a special case of the cube-connected cycles ([Prep81]), they are called the base-m n-level cube-connected cycles in [Anne87].

When we compare the braid graphs $b(R(n), U, i \; \mathbf{mod} \; s)$ with the cartesian product graphs $R(n) \times U^s$ we obtain some remarkable results. Consider, for instance, $2 \le s \le n \; \mathbf{div} \; 4 + 1$. Comparing the degree and the diameter, we find for $b(R(n), U, i \; \mathbf{mod} \; s)$

$$d = 2 + d_U \text{ and } k = n \text{ div } 2 + s \cdot k_U \,,$$

whereas, for $G \times U^s$,

$$d = 2 + s \cdot d_U \text{ and } k = n \text{ div } 2 + s \cdot k_U \,.$$

Hence the graphs have the same number of vertices, the same diameter, whilst the degree of the braid graph is an order of magnitude smaller than the degree of the corresponding cartesian product graph.

Next we compute the beneficial effects of this lower degree on the width of an edge. Assume $n = |G.V|$ and $m = |U.V|$ to be even. According to the following formula for the bisection width for the cartesian product graph $G \times U$

$$B(G \times U) \leq m \cdot B(G) \text{ min } n \cdot B(U) \,,$$

we find

$$B(G \times U^s) \leq m^s \cdot B(G) \text{ min } n \cdot m^{s-1} \cdot B(U) \,.$$

Again we assume that equality holds. For $G = R(n)$ we then have

$$B = \begin{cases} 2 \cdot m^s \text{ min } n \cdot m^{s-1} B(U), & \text{for } R(n) \times U^s \,, \\ 2 \cdot m^s \text{ min } \frac{n}{s} \cdot m^{s-1} B(U), & \text{for } b(R(n), U, i \text{ mod } s) \,. \end{cases}$$

Hence, when $n \cdot B(U) \leq 2 \cdot m$, the edges of $b(R(n), U, i \text{ mod } s)$ will be s times as wide as the edges of $R(n) \times U^s$. As we shall see these relatively wide edges make the braid graphs $b(R(n), U, i \text{ mod } s)$ attractive candidates for processor networks, when latency is considered. Recall(see section 2.3) that we have defined the latency of a processor by

$$T = (\frac{L}{W} + \overline{RA}) \cdot T_c \,,$$

where $\overline{RA}$ denotes the average length of a path when routing algorithm RA is used, and T_c denotes the edge delay. Hence in order to determine the latency of a graph-connected ring a routing algorithm is necessary. Determining a shortest path routing algorithm appears to be an awkward problem. At least some case analysis seems necessary. Let x be a vertex of U, and let u denote the element of $U.V^A$ satisfying $\forall (i : 0 \leq i < s : u(i) = x)$. Consider the construction of a shortest path from $(0, u)$ to (h, v). As we have shown in section 3.2 we should determine a shortest path $p(i : 0 \leq i \leq r)$ in $R(n)$ such that $p(0) = 0, p(r) = h$, and $D(u, v) \subseteq \{i : 0 \leq i \leq r : p(i) \text{ mod } s\}$. Consider, for instance, $n = 12, h = 2$, and assume $v(1) \neq x \wedge v(s-1) \neq x$. When $s = 12$, a shortest path is $0, 11, 0, 1, 2$, but when $s = 3$

the path $0, 1, 2$ should be chosen. Instead of considering all these cases we take a simpler approach by presenting an alternative routing algorithm RA which does not necessarily give shortest paths, but the length of a path established by RA does not exceed the diameter of $b(R(n), U, i \bmod s)$.

In describing the alternative routing algorithm for a path from (g, w) to (h, v) we restrict ourselves to the case $(g, w) = (0, u)$, where u satisfies $\forall (i : 0 \leq i < s : u(i) = x)$. Due to the vertex-transitivity of $b(R(n), U, i \bmod s)$ similar descriptions can be given for all other vertices. A path $p(u, v)(i : 0 \leq i \leq q)$ is called a difference-set-complete path of (u, v) if $D(u, v) \subseteq \{i : 0 \leq i \leq q : p(u, v)(i) \bmod s\}$. In general, several shortest difference-set-complete paths may exist. In order to simplify the analysis only one difference-set-complete path is determined by the algorithm. Define the subsets $S(n)$ and $H(n)$ of $R(n).V$ by

$$S(n) = \{h : 0 \leq h < (n+1) \textbf{ div } 2 : h\}, \text{ and } H(n) = \{h : (n+1) \textbf{ div } 2 \leq h < n : h\}.$$

Next we distinguish between two cases, viz. $1 \leq s \leq n \textbf{ div } 2$ and $s = n$.

- $1 \leq s \leq n \textbf{ div } 2$.

  For $(h, v) \in S(n) \times (U.V)^A$ the difference-set-complete path $p(u, v)(i : 0 \leq i \leq q)$ is the path in a "clockwise direction" satisfying

  $$p(u, v)(i) = i, \text{ for all } i, \ 0 \leq i \leq q, \text{ and}$$

  $$q = \textbf{MAX}(i : 0 \leq i < s \wedge v(i) \neq x : i) \textbf{ max } 0,$$

  and for $(h, v) \in H(n) \times (U.V)^A$ it is the path in a "anticlockwise direction", such that

  $$p(u, v)(i) = (n - i) \bmod n, \text{ for all } i, 0 \leq i \leq q, \text{ and}$$

  $$q = \textbf{MAX}(i : 1 \leq i < s \wedge v(i) \neq x : s - i) \textbf{ max } 0 .$$

- $s = n$

  The only adjustment from the former case is to reverse directions.

The remaining G-part of a path in $b(R(n), U, i \bmod s)$ from $(0, u)$ to (h, v) corresponds to a shortest path in G from the terminal vertex of the difference-set-complete path $p(u, v)$ to h. The U-part of the routing algorithm described in section 3.2 is not changed. Hence, for $(h, v) \in S(n) \times (U.V)^A$, $1 \leq s \leq n \textbf{ div } 2$, and $q = \textbf{MAX}(i : 0 \leq i < s \wedge v(i) \neq x : i) \textbf{ max } 0$, the routing algorithm reads

$(l, w) := (0, u)$
;   **do** $l < q \rightarrow shp\_in\_U(w(l \bmod s)), v(l \bmod s))$
         ; $(l, w) := (l + 1, w)$
  od
; $shp\_in\_U(w(l \bmod s)), v(l \bmod s))$ $\{w = v\}$
;   **do** $l < h \rightarrow (l, w) := (l + 1, w)$
; $[\!]$ $l > h \rightarrow (l, w) := (l - 1, w)$
  od
  $\{(l, w) = (h, v)\}$

where l and w are variables from $R(n).V$ and $(U.V)^A$, respectively, and shp_in_U is the procedure specified in section 3.2. An invariant of the first loop is

$$\forall(i : 0 \leq i < l : w(i) = v(i)) \wedge 0 \leq l \leq q$$

whereas *true* is an invariant of the second loop. A similar algorithm can be given for $(h, v) \in H(n) \times (U.V)^A$ and $1 \leq s \leq n \text{ div } 2$.

When $s = n$ the above algorithm needs some adjustments, mainly in the last **do-od** construction, since a shortest path in G from the terminal vertex of a difference-set-complete path to h can have either direction. For $(h, v) \in S(n) \times (U.V)^A$, $s = n$, and $q = \mathbf{MAX}(i : 1 \leq i < s \wedge v(i) \neq 0 : s - i) \mathbf{\ max\ } 0$, the algorithm reads

$aq := (n - q) \bmod n$; $(l, w) := (0, u)$
;   **do** $l \neq q \rightarrow shp\_in\_U(w(l)), v(l))$
         ; $(l, w) := ((l - 1) \bmod n, w)$
  od
; $shp\_in\_U(w(l)), v(l))$ $\{w = v\}$
;   **if** $l \leq h \rightarrow le := h - l$; $ri := n + l - h$
; $[\!]$ $l \geq h \rightarrow le := n + h - l$; $ri := l - h$
  fi
;   **if** $le \leq ri \rightarrow$ **do** $l \neq h \rightarrow (l, w) := ((l + 1) \bmod n, w)$ **od**
; $[\!]$ $le \geq ri \rightarrow$ **do** $l \neq h \rightarrow (l, w) := ((l - 1) \bmod n, w)$ **od**
  fi
  $\{(l, w) = (h, v)\}$

where aq is a variable from $R(n).V$ denoting the terminal vertex of the difference-set-complete path, and, le and ri denote the length of a shortest path in $R(n)$ from aq to h in clockwise and anticlockwise directions, respectively.

Next we explain why we have chosen to let the ring be traversed in an anticlockwise direction for $h \in S(n)$ and $s = n$.

Property 3.33
The average number of "indices" in which u and v differ is

$$s \cdot \frac{m-1}{m}.$$

Proof
The (success) probability that an element of $U.V$ differs from x is $\frac{m-1}{m}$. The average number of successes in s independent experiments with success probability p in each experiment equals $s \cdot p$. Hence, on average u and v will differ in $s \cdot \frac{m-1}{m}$ indices. (End of proof and property)

From this property it follows that, when $s = n$, on average u and v will differ in $n \cdot \frac{m-1}{m}$ indices. Hence, the average length of a difference-set-complete path will be larger than n **div** 2, for only if u and v differ in precisely the first $n \cdot \frac{m-1}{m}$ indices is a path of length $n \cdot \frac{m-1}{m} - 1$ established. Consequently, when routing in an anticlockwise direction is chosen for $h \in S(n)$, the average distance between h and the terminal vertex of a difference-set-complete path will be small.

Our next issue concerns the average length $\overline{RA}$ of a path established by a routing algorithm RA. Similarly as in section 3.2 we distinguish between the $R(n)$-part and the U-part of a path. We start with the latter.

Property 3.34
The average length of the U-part of a path established by RA is $s \cdot \overline{k_U}$.

Proof
The average length of a shortest path in U from x to y, with $x \neq y$, is

$$\frac{\mathbf{S}(y : y \in U.V \wedge x \neq y : k_U(x,y))}{m-1}.$$

Since $\overline{k_U} = \frac{\mathbf{S}(y:y \in U.V:k_U(x,y))}{m}$ and $k_U(x,x) = 0$, the average length of a shortest path in U from x to y, with $x \neq y$, is $\frac{m}{m-1} \cdot \overline{k_U}$. According to property 3.33 on average u and v will differ in $s \cdot \frac{m-1}{m}$ indices. Hence, the average length of the U-part is $s \cdot \frac{m-1}{m} \cdot \frac{m}{m-1} \cdot \overline{k_U} = s \cdot \overline{k_U}$.
(End of proof and property)

Next, we calculate the average length of the $R(n)$-part of a path established by RA. It is the sum of the average length of a difference-set-complete path and the average distance between the terminal vertex of such a path and a vertex of G. First we consider the average length of a difference-set-complete path. Let Y be the length of a difference-set-complete path that is established by the routing algorithm RA. For the sake of simplicity we assume that routing in the clockwise direction is used, but by permuting the indices equal results can be obtained for routing in the anticlockwise direction.

Property 3.35

$$\overline{Y} = s - \frac{m}{m-1} + \frac{1}{m^{s-1}(m-1)} \,.$$

Proof

The probability that Y equals q, with $0 < q < s$, is

$P(Y = q)$
$=$ { def. of the routing algorithm }
$\frac{1}{m^s} \cdot \mathbf{N}(v : v \in U.V^A : \mathbf{MAX}(i : 0 \le i < s \wedge v(i) \ne x : i) \text{ max } 0 = q)$
$=$ { calculus }
$\frac{1}{m^s} \cdot m^q \cdot (m-1)$.

Hence

$\overline{Y}$
$=$ { def. of average }
$\mathbf{S}(q : 0 \le q < s : q \cdot P(Y = q))$

$=$

$\mathbf{S}(q : 1 \le q < s : q \cdot \frac{1}{m^s} \cdot m^q(m-1))$
$=$ { calculus }
$\frac{m \cdot (m-1)}{m^s} \cdot \frac{(s-1)m^s - s \cdot m^{s-1} + 1}{(m-1)^2}$
$=$ { calculus }
$s - \frac{m}{m-1} + \frac{1}{m^{s-1}(m-1)}$.

(End of proof and property)

So on average between $s-2$ and $s-1$ edges are traversed to establish a difference-set-complete path. If we consider the cube-connected cycles, $b(R(n), K(2), id)$, we have $s = n$ and $m = 2$, and, hence, the average length of a difference-set-complete path in $b(R(n), K(2), id)$ is $n - 2 + \frac{1}{2^{n-1}}$.

Remark 3.36

This average case analysis justifies our choice to use a ring for G. In fact, shortest difference-set-complete paths would be obtained by choosing a complete graph $G = K(n)$. In that case, the same methods as above would yield an average value

$$(s-1) \cdot \frac{m-1}{m} = s - 1 - \frac{s-1}{m}.$$

Hence, when s is at most m, the average length of a difference-set-complete path in $b(K(n), U, i \bmod s)$ will also between $s - 2$ and $s - 1$. The main reason why a near optimal value is obtained for a ring is that a ring has a path of minimal length in which all vertices have a different modulo s value.

Since the other term of the average length $\overline{RA}$ we have determined, viz. $s \cdot \overline{k}_U$, is independent of G, the real difference between the average distance of $b(R(n), U, i \bmod s)$ and $b(K(n), U, i \bmod s)$ is the average length of a shortest path from the terminal vertex of a difference-set-complete path to a vertex of G. For $G = K(n)$ it is $\overline{k}_G = \frac{n-1}{n}$, but, for $G = R(n), \overline{k}_G = \frac{n}{4}$ is an upper bound due to the high probability that the terminal vertex of a difference-set-complete path and the destination vertex are near each other.

(End of remark)

Next, we calculate the average distance $\overline{l}$ between the terminal vertex of a difference-set-complete path and the destination vertex as follows.

Since the routing algorithm differs for the vertex sets $S(n)$ and $H(n)$, $\overline{l}$ also has two components. Let $\overline{l}_S$ be the average distance when routing in $S(n)$ is considered, and similarly for $\overline{l}_H$ and $H(n)$. We first consider $\overline{l}_S$. It is given by

$$\overline{l}_S = \mathbf{S}(g : 0 \leq g < n : P(Z_S = g) \cdot k_S(g)),$$

where $P(Z_S = g)$ denotes the probability that g is the terminal vertex of a difference-set-complete path with initial vertex 0, and $k_S(g)$ is given by

$$k_S(g) = \frac{\mathbf{S}(h : h \in S(n) : k_G(g, h))}{|S(n)|}.$$

Similarly as in the calculation of the average length $\overline{Y}$ of a difference-set-complete path we have

$$P(Z_S = 0) = \frac{m}{m^s},$$
$$P(Z_S = g) = 0, \qquad \text{for } s \leq g < n,$$
$$P(Z_S = g) = \frac{(m-1)m^g}{m^s}, \qquad \text{for } 1 \leq s \leq n \text{ div } 2 \wedge 1 \leq g < s, \text{ and}$$
$$P(Z_S = g) = \frac{(m-1)m^{n-g}}{m^n}, \qquad \text{for } s = n \wedge 1 \leq g < n,$$

since for $1 \leq s \leq n$ **div** 2 clockwise routing and for $s = n$ anticlockwise routing is used. So it remains to calculate $k_S(g)$ for $0 \leq g < s$. For the sake of simplicity we assume n to be even. For odd n only small changes are needed. Next, as might be expected, we distinguish between $1 \leq s \leq \frac{n}{2}$ and $s = n$.

When $1 \leq s \leq \frac{n}{2}$, a shortest path in the ring $R(n)$ from g to h, with $0 \leq g < s$ and $0 \leq h < \frac{n}{2}$, corresponds to a shortest path in the linear array graph $P(\frac{n}{2})$. Hence

$$k_G(g, h) = (g - h) \; \mathbf{max} \; (h - g).$$

Property 3.37
For $0 \leq g < s \; \wedge \; 1 \leq s \leq \frac{n}{2}$ we have

$$k_S(g) = \frac{2 \cdot g \cdot (g + 1)}{n} + \frac{1}{2} \cdot \left(\frac{n}{2} - (2g + 1) \right).$$

Proof

$k_S(g)$

$=$ { def. of k_S, $S(n) = \{h : 0 \leq h < \frac{n}{2} : h\}$ }

    $\frac{2}{n} \cdot \mathbf{S}(h : 0 \leq h < \frac{n}{2} : (g - h) \; \mathbf{max} \; (h - g))$

$=$ { calculus }

    $\frac{2}{n} \cdot \mathbf{S}(h : 0 \leq h \leq g : g - h) + \frac{2}{n} \cdot \mathbf{S}(h : g < h < \frac{n}{2} : h - g)$

$=$ { calculus }

    $\frac{2}{n} \cdot \mathbf{S}(h : 0 \leq h \leq g : h) + \frac{2}{n} \cdot \mathbf{S}(h : 0 < h < \frac{n}{2} - g : h)$

$=$ { calculus }

    $\frac{2}{n} \cdot \frac{1}{2} \cdot g \cdot (g + 1) + \frac{2}{n} \cdot \frac{1}{2} \cdot (\frac{n}{2} - g - 1) \cdot (\frac{n}{2} - g)$

$=$ { calculus }

    $\frac{2 \cdot g \cdot (g+1)}{n} + \frac{1}{2} \cdot (\frac{n}{2} - (2g + 1))$.

(End of proof and property)

From this formula for $k_S(g)$ we compute $\bar{l}_S$.

Property 3.38

For $1 \leq s \leq \frac{n}{2}$ we have

$$\bar{l}_s \simeq \frac{1}{2}(\frac{n}{2} - 1) + \frac{2s(s-1)}{n} - \frac{4(s-1)}{n \cdot (m-1)} - (s - \frac{m}{m-1}),$$

where $\simeq$ denotes "is approximately".

Proof

$\bar{l}_s$

$=$ { def. of $\bar{l}_s$ }

$\mathbf{S}(g : 0 \leq g < s : P(Z_s = g) \cdot k_s(g))$

$=$ { formulae for $P(Z_s = g)$ and $k_s(g)$ }

$\frac{m}{m^s} \cdot \frac{1}{2}(\frac{n}{2} - 1) + \mathbf{S}(g : 1 \leq g < s : \frac{(m-1)m^g}{m^s} \cdot (\frac{2 \cdot g \cdot (g+1)}{n} + \frac{1}{2}(\frac{n}{2} - (2g+1))))$

$=$ { calculus }

$\frac{m}{2 \cdot m^s} \cdot (\frac{n}{2} - 1) + \frac{2 \cdot (m-1)m}{n \cdot m^s} \cdot \mathbf{S}(g : 1 \leq g < s : g(g+1) \cdot m^{g-1}) +$

$\frac{m-1}{2 \cdot m^s} \cdot (\frac{n}{2} - 1) \cdot \mathbf{S}(g : 1 \leq g < s : m^g) - \frac{(m-1) \cdot m}{m^s} \cdot \mathbf{S}(g : 1 \leq g < s : g \cdot m^{g-1}).$

Since

$\mathbf{S}(g : 1 \leq g < s : g(g+1)m^{g-1})$

$=$ { calculus }

$\frac{d^2}{dm^2}(\mathbf{S}(g : 1 \leq g < s : m^{g+1}))$

$=$ { calculus }

$\frac{d^2}{dm^2}(\frac{m^{s+1}-1}{m-1} - 1 - m)$

$=$ { calculus }

$\frac{s(s+1)m^{s-1}}{m-1} - \frac{2sm^s}{(m-1)^2} + \frac{2(m^s-1)}{(m-1)^3},$

$\mathbf{S}(g : 1 \leq g < s : m^g) = \frac{m^s - m}{m-1}$, and

$\mathbf{S}(g : 1 \leq g < s : g \cdot m^{g-1})$

$=$ { calculus }

$\frac{d}{dm}(\mathbf{S}(g : 1 \leq g < s : m^g))$

$=$ { calculus }

$\frac{s \cdot m^{s-1}}{m-1} - \frac{m^s}{(m-1)^2} + \frac{1}{(m-1)^2},$

we obtain for $\bar{l}_s$ the following formula:

$$\bar{l}_S = \frac{m}{2 \cdot m^s} \cdot \left(\frac{n}{2} - 1\right) + \frac{2s(s+1)}{n} - \frac{4m \cdot s}{n \cdot (m-1)} + \frac{4m}{n \cdot (m-1)^2} - \frac{4m}{n \cdot m^s (m-1)^2} +$$
$$\frac{(m^s - m)}{2 \cdot m^s} \left(\frac{n}{2} - 1\right) - \left(s - \frac{m}{m-1} + \frac{1}{m^{s-1}(m-1)}\right).$$

Ignoring two small terms this formula reduces to

$$\bar{l}_S \simeq \frac{1}{2}\left(\frac{n}{2} - 1\right) + \frac{2s(s-1)}{n} - \frac{4(s-1)}{n \cdot (m-1)} - \left(s - \frac{m}{m-1}\right).$$

(End of proof and property)

We have included this analysis to show that the formula

$$\frac{2(s-1)^2}{n} + \frac{1}{2}\left(\frac{n}{2} - 1\right) - \left(s - \frac{3}{2}\right)$$

is a good estimate for $\bar{l}_S$. It can be derived as follows. According to property 3.33 on average between $s - 2$ and $s - 1$ edges are traversed to establish a difference-set-complete path. We could estimate $\bar{l}_S$ by

$$\bar{l}_S \simeq \frac{1}{2}\left(k_S(s - 2) + k_S(s - 1)\right).$$

Using property 3.37 this results in

$$\bar{l}_S \simeq \frac{2(s-1)^2}{n} + \frac{1}{2}\left(\frac{n}{2} - 1\right) - \left(s - \frac{3}{2}\right).$$

Due to the reductions applied to obtain the first formula for $\bar{l}_S$, we conclude that the second formula indeed is a good estimate. We prefer the simpler of the two estimates for $\bar{l}_S$. Hence,

Property 3.39
For $1 \le s \le n$ **div** 2 we have

$$\bar{l}_S \simeq \frac{2(s-1)^2}{n} + \frac{n}{4} - (s - 1).$$

(End of property)

On account of these results we consider for $s = n$ the simple approach only. The terminal vertices of the difference-set-complete paths of length $s - 2$ and $s - 1$ are 2 and 1, respectively. Hence we have for $s = n$ and $n \ge 3$

$$\bar{l}_S \simeq \frac{1}{2}\left(k_S(2) + k_S(1)\right).$$

Using property 3.37 again, it follows that

Property 3.40

For $s = n$ we have

$$\bar{l}_S = \frac{8}{n} + \frac{n}{4} - 2 .$$

(End of property)

Notice that the formulae for $\bar{l}_S$ are estimates. For small $s, m,$ or n straight calculation might be preferred.

Using similar derivations we can determine $\bar{l}_H$. Although sets $S(n)$ and $H(n)$ are not equivalent with respect to RA, $\bar{l}_S$ and $\bar{l}_H$ will not differ much. We therefore use the estimate of $\bar{l}_S$ for the average distance $\bar{l}$ between the terminal vertex of a difference-set-complete path and the destination vertex.

After this long analysis we collect the results derived to achieve the average length $\overline{RA}$ of $b(R(n), U, \alpha)$.

Theorem 3.41

$$\overline{RA} \simeq \begin{cases} \frac{2(s-1)^2}{n} + \frac{n}{4} + s \cdot \overline{k}_U & \text{for } 1 \leq s \leq n \textbf{ div } 2 , \\ n + \frac{n}{4} - 3 + \frac{8}{n} + s \cdot \overline{k}_U & \text{for } s = n . \end{cases}$$

Proof

For $1 \leq s \leq n$ **div** 2 we have

$\overline{RA}$

$=$ { def. of $\overline{RA}$ }

$\bar{l} + \overline{Y} + s \cdot \overline{k}_U$

$\simeq$ { property 3.35 and property 3.39 }

$(\frac{2(s-1)^2}{n} + \frac{n}{4} - (s-1)) + (s - \frac{m}{m-1} + \frac{1}{m^{s-1}(m-1)}) + s \cdot \overline{k}_U$

$\simeq$

$\frac{2(s-1)^2}{n} + \frac{n}{4} + s \cdot \overline{k}_U ,$

and, for $s = n,$

$$\overline{RA}$$
$$\simeq \quad \{ \text{ property 3.40 } \}$$
$$\left(\tfrac{8}{n} + \tfrac{n}{4} - 2\right) + \left(n - \tfrac{m}{m-1} + \tfrac{1}{m^{s-1}(m-1)}\right) + s \cdot \overline{k}_U$$
$$\simeq$$
$$n + \tfrac{n}{4} - 3 + \tfrac{8}{n} + s \cdot \overline{k}_U \, .$$

(End of proof and theorem)

In the analysis we have also determined the average distance $\overline{k}$ of $b(K(n), U, i \bmod s)$,

$$\overline{k} = (s-1) \cdot \frac{m-1}{m} + \frac{n-1}{n} + s \cdot \overline{k}_U \simeq s + s \cdot \overline{k}_U \, ,$$

so the main difference is the average distance $\tfrac{n}{4}$ of $R(n)$.

Equipped with the average distance and the width of the edges we can determine the latency of $b(R(n), U, i \bmod s)$,

$$T = T_c \cdot \left(\frac{L}{W} + \overline{RA}\right).$$

We begin by considering the edge delay T_c to be constant.

Example 3.42

We consider the latency of braid graphs $b(G, U, i \bmod s)$ with 2^{12} vertices, and compare it with the latency of a k-ary n-cube that has the same number of vertices, i.e., $k^n = 2^{12}$. For comparison reasons G is allowed to be either a ring or a complete graph.

Assuming $T_c = 1$ and $L = 128$ we conclude from example 2.2 that the lowest latency of a k-ary n-cube with 2^{12} vertices is obtained for $k = 64$ and $n = 2$. This torus has latency 36. Next we consider several braid graphs. In the beginning of this section we derived the following formula for the width of an edge of $b(G, U, i \bmod s)$:

$$W = \frac{n}{B(G)} \max \frac{m \cdot s}{B(U)} \, .$$

From $n \cdot m^s = 2^{12}, s/n$, and, $s > 1$ we infer $n > 2$ and $s = 2, 4$, or 8.

- $s = 8$.

    When $s = 8$, we have $n = 16$ and $m = 2$. Hence, $B(U) = 1$ and $\overline{k}_U = \tfrac{1}{2}$, and since $B(G) > 1$ the width of an edge is 16. For $G = R(16)$, we find $\overline{RA} \simeq 14$, and hence $T \simeq 1 \cdot (8+14) = 22$. Although, due to the large degree, a complete graph with 16 vertices is not amenable, we give the result for $G = K(16)$ to show that by choosing any other starred polygon with 16 vertices the difference is small. Using $\overline{k} = (s-1) \cdot \frac{m-1}{m} + \frac{n-1}{n} + s \cdot \overline{k}_U$ we obtain $T \simeq 1 \cdot (8+8\frac{1}{2}) = 16\frac{1}{2}$.

- $s = 4$.

If $s = 4$, then $m = 2$ and $m = 4$ are possible. For $m = 2$ we have $n = 256$, and by choosing $G = R(256)$ we obtain $W = 128$ and $\overline{RA} \simeq 66$, and, hence, $T \simeq 67$. If $m = 4$, then again we have $n = 16$. For U there are two possibilities, viz. $U = R(4)$ or $U = K(4)$. We obtain for $b(R(16), R(4), i \bmod 4)$, $W = 8$ and by using $\overline{RA} \simeq \frac{2(s-1)^2}{n} + \frac{n}{4} + s \cdot \overline{k}_U$, $T \simeq 1 \cdot (16 + 9\frac{1}{2}) = 25\frac{1}{2}$.

For $G = K(16)$ and $U = R(4)$ the latency is approximately 24, and graph $b(K(16), K(4), i \bmod 4)$ has $W = \frac{4 \cdot 4}{4} = 4$, $\overline{k} \simeq 7$, and $T \simeq 39$.

The remaining case $G = R(16)$ and $U = K(4)$ leads to $W = 8$, $\overline{RA} \simeq 8\frac{1}{2}$, and, hence, the latency of $b(R(16), K(4), i \bmod 4)$ is approximately $24\frac{1}{2}$.

- $s = 2$.

When $s = 2$, then we have numerous possibilities for G and U. From the above cases for $s = 4$ and $s = 8$ we may conclude that it is reasonable to assume that G is a ring graph. Instead of considering all remaining possibilities when G is a ring graph, we restrict our attention to braid graphs with a latency less than 32. Due to the factor $\frac{n}{4}$ in the average distance we thus have $n = 4, n = 16$, or $n = 64$. We start with the last. If $n = 64$ then we have $m = 8$. Choosing $U = R(8)$ we obtain for $b(R(64), U, i \bmod 2)$, $W = 32$ and $\overline{RA} \simeq 20$, hence $T \simeq 24$. When we consider $b(R(64), K(8), i \bmod 2)$ we get $T \simeq 22$.

For $n = 16$ we obtain $m = 16$, so we can vary U to obtain several low latency braid graphs. Choosing $B(U) = 2$, i.e., $U = R(16)$, leads to $W = 16$, $\overline{RA} \simeq 12$, and $T \simeq 20$. The following choice of U shows that applying the braid operation more than once can also give good results. Consider $U = b(R(4)), K(2), i \bmod 2)$. Then U is the braid graph depicted in figure 3.3. U satisfies $B(U) = 4$ and $\overline{RA}_U = 2\frac{1}{4}$. So in this case we have $W = 8$, $\overline{RA} \simeq 8\frac{1}{2}$, and, hence, $T = 24\frac{1}{2}$.

When $n = 4$, then we have even more possibilities for U. We select two of them, viz. $U = R(32)$ and $U = b(K(2), R(4), id)$. The former leads to a braid graph with wide edges, viz. $W = 32$, and a relatively large average distance, viz. $\overline{RA} = 17\frac{1}{2}$, resulting in a low latency of $21\frac{1}{2}$. For $U = b(K(2), R(4), id)$ we have $B(U) = 8$ and $\overline{RA}_U = 3$. So, $b(R(4), U, i \bmod 2)$ has $W = 8, \overline{RA} = 7\frac{1}{2}$, and, hence, a latency of $23\frac{1}{2}$.

The above results are summarized in the following table.

G	U	s	$T \simeq$
$R(16)$	$R(2)$	8	22
$K(16)$	$R(2)$	8	$16\frac{1}{2}$
$R(256)$	$R(2)$	4	67
$R(16)$	$R(4)$	4	$25\frac{1}{2}$
$R(16)$	$K(4)$	4	$24\frac{1}{2}$
$K(16)$	$R(4)$	4	24
$K(16)$	$K(4)$	4	39
$R(64)$	$R(8)$	2	24
$R(64)$	$K(8)$	2	22
$R(16)$	$R(16)$	2	20
$R(16)$	$b(R(4), K(2), i \bmod 2)$	2	$24\frac{1}{2}$
$R(4)$	$R(32)$	2	$21\frac{1}{2}$
$R(4)$	$b(K(2), R(4), id)$	2	$24\frac{1}{2}$

We have included this long list of braid graphs for at least three reasons.

First, to show that with the braid operation a large variety of low latency graphs can be constructed. This low latency results from the property that the braid graph of two small degree graphs is again a small degree graph. Most of the braid graphs considered in this example have degree 4 or 5. As in Chapter 2 this affirms that small degree networks achieve lower latency than large degree ones. Second, to show that the impact of the value of s on the latency is small. In all three cases of s, braid graphs exist with a latency of approximately 20. A small s, however, has the additional advantage that G and U can be varied. The third reason is to show that the latency is low when both G and U are ring graphs. Neglecting the case $G = K(16)$, in this example the lowest latencies are achieved by choosing $G = R(16)$ and $U = R(16)$ and by $G = R(4)$ and $U = R(32)$. Notice that in both cases $s = 2$ holds.
(End of example)

In the example above we compared braid graphs with k-ary n-cubes. In order to show that the results obtained are impressive we compare in the next two examples braid graphs with two other important classes of graphs, viz. binary trees and grids.

Example 3.43

In this example we calculate the latency of a complete binary tree. First we consider the average distance. For a complete binary tree with $2^n - 1$ vertices the average distance $\bar{k}$ is $\frac{1}{(2^n-1)^2}((2n - 6)2^{2n} + (n + 3)2^{n+1})$.

It is obvious that a complete binary tree with at least three vertices has bisection width 1. So, when n is sufficiently large and L is relatively small, $\frac{L}{w} + \bar{k} \simeq 2n - 6$. Hence a complete binary tree with $2^{12} - 1$ vertices has a slightly better latency than the braid graphs described in example 3.42, when edge delay is neglected. A binary tree, however, has a deficiency concerning the latency. When messages are uniformly distributed over the vertices, the load is very unequally distributed over the edges. On account of the average distance almost all messages have to pass through the root or the vertices immediately below the root. Hence, the edges incident to these vertices are extensively used, whereas edges incident to the leaves are hardly used. When we consider, for instance, a braid graph $b(R(n), R(m), i \bmod 2)$, then we have

$$\overline{RA}$$
$$=$$
$$(2 \cdot \frac{(s-1)^2}{n} + \frac{n}{4} - (s - 1) + s - \frac{m}{m-1} + \frac{1}{m^{s-1}(m-1)}) + s \cdot \overline{k}_U$$
$$= \quad \{ s = 2, \overline{k}_U = \frac{m}{4} \}$$
$$(\frac{2}{n} + \frac{n}{4} + 1 - (\frac{m-1}{m-1} + \frac{1}{m-1}) + (\frac{1}{m-1} - \frac{1}{m})) + \frac{m}{2}$$
$$=$$
$$(\frac{2}{n} + \frac{n}{4} - \frac{1}{m}) + \frac{m}{2},$$

so on average approximately $\frac{n}{4}$ edges of $R(n)$ and $\frac{m}{2}$ edges of $R(m)$ are used. According to proposition 3.7.(iii) there are $n \cdot m^2$ $R(n)$-edges and $n \cdot m^2$ $R(m)$-edges in $b(R(n), R(m), i \bmod 2)$. Hence, the average message density per $R(n)$-edge in this braid graph is $\frac{\frac{n}{4} \cdot nm^2}{n \cdot m^2} = \frac{n}{4}$, and, similarly, $\frac{m}{2}$ for a $R(m)$-edge. The vertex-transitivity of the braid graph implies that there are no exceptional vertices which consume a major part of the message traffic. Hence, when m and n are not too different, the load is evenly distributed over the edges of $b(R(n), R(m), i \bmod 2)$.
(End of example)

Example 3.44

Grid graphs, in particular square grids, form another class of graphs that are frequently used as processor networks. In this example we compute the latency of a grid, and compare the result with the latencies of the braid graphs of example 3.42. We assume that a shortest path routing algorithm is used.

A grid graph $GR(n)$ is the cartesian product graph of two linear array graphs $P(l)$ and $P(m)$. For the sake of simplicity l and m are assumed to be even. We have for the bisection width of $GR(n)$

$$B(GR(n)) = m \cdot B(P(l)) \ \mathbf{min} \ l \cdot B(P(m)) .$$

For the average distance we have

$$\overline{k}_{GR(n)} = \overline{k}_{P(l)} + \overline{k}_{P(m)} .$$

Since the bisection width of a linear array is 1, it suffices to determine the average distance of a linear array to obtain the latency of a grid. Unfortunately $P(l)$ is not distance-regular, so we have to compute

$$\overline{k} = \frac{\mathbf{S}(x, y : 0 \leq x, y < l : k(x,y))}{l^2} .$$

In property 3.37 we have already determined $\mathbf{S}(y : 0 \leq y < l : k(x,y))$ for a vertex x of $P(l)$. It is $x(x+1) + \frac{1}{2}(l^2 - (2x+1) \cdot l)$, so $\overline{k}$ is

$$
\begin{aligned}
&\overline{k} \\
=\quad &\{ \text{ calculus } \} \\
&\tfrac{1}{l^2} \cdot \mathbf{S}(x : 0 \leq x < l : x(x+1)) + \tfrac{1}{l} \cdot \mathbf{S}(x : 0 \leq x < l : \tfrac{1}{2}(l - (2x+1))) \\
=\quad &\{ \ \mathbf{S}(x : 0 \leq x < l : l - (2x+1)) = 0 \ \} \\
&\tfrac{1}{l^2}\mathbf{S}(x : 0 \leq x < l : x^2) + \tfrac{1}{l^2}\mathbf{S}(x : 0 \leq x < l : x) \\
=\quad &\{ \text{ calculus } \} \\
&\tfrac{1}{l^2}(\tfrac{1}{6} \cdot (l-1) \cdot l \cdot (2l-1) + \tfrac{1}{2} \cdot (l-1) \cdot l) \\
=\quad & \\
&\tfrac{1}{3}(l-1) \cdot l \cdot (l+1) \cdot \tfrac{1}{l^2} \\
\simeq\quad & \\
&\tfrac{1}{3}l .
\end{aligned}
$$

Assuming $l \leq m$ and according to $B \cdot W = l \cdot m$ we thus obtain

$$
\begin{aligned}
&T \\
=\quad &\{ \text{ def. of } T \text{ with } T_c = 1 \ \} \\
&\tfrac{L}{W} + \overline{k} \\
=\quad & \\
&\tfrac{L}{m} + \tfrac{1}{3}(l+m) .
\end{aligned}
$$

In particular, if $L = 128$ and $l \cdot m = 2^{12}$, we have $T > \frac{1}{3}(2^6 + 2^6) \simeq 42$. Hence, several braid graphs of example 3.42 have a lower latency, at least when we assume that edge delay is constant.
(End of example)

From these three examples we conclude that under the assumption of constant edge delay braid graphs can be constructed with a low latency. Next, this assumption is released. As we showed in Chapter 2, the delay of an edge depends on its length; so we are interested in braid graphs with short edges. When we regard $b(R(n), U, i \bmod s)$ as $|U.V|^s$ copies of $R(n)$, this means that for each ring the number of copies with which it has a connection should be small. Consider a vertex of a ring. It has exactly d_U (U-)edges with vertices of other rings. Hence each ring is connected with $s \cdot d_U$ other rings. So to keep the edges short $s \cdot d_U$ must be small. An interesting case appears if we choose $s = 2$ and $d_U = 2$. These graphs $b(G, R(m), i \bmod 2)$ are the topic of the next section.

3.5 Torus-connected graphs

In this section we consider the braid graphs $b(G, R(m), \alpha)$ with graph G and function α such that α is a surjective mapping from $G.V$ to $\{0, 1\}$ and G is α-vertex-transitive. We further assume that m is at least 3.

Example 3.45

Let G be the graph $R(4)$ and $m = 3$. Apart from isomorphism there are two possible values for α, viz. $\alpha(i) = i \bmod 2$ and $\alpha(i) = i \mathbf{div}\ 2$. The braid graphs corresponding to these α's are depicted in figures 3.46 and 3.47.

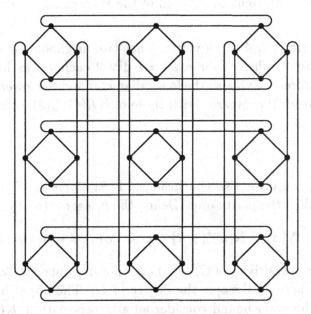

Figure 3.46: $b(R(4), R(3), i \bmod 2)$

The graph $b(R(4), R(3), i \bmod 2)$ has 36 vertices, degree 4, and diameter 4. The bisection width is 18, which is relatively large due to the odd parity of m. Straight calculation shows that the average distance is $2\frac{2}{3}$.

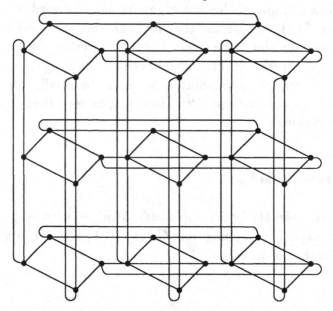

Figure 3.47: $b(R(4), R(3), i \textbf{ div } 2)$

The graph $b(R(4), R(3), i \textbf{ div } 2)$ has 36 vertices, degree 4, and bisection width 18, but it has diameter 5. Straight calculation of the average distance gives the value 3.

Notice that in the graph $R(4)$ each vertex g has two neighbours h with $\alpha(g) \neq \alpha(h)$ when $\alpha(i) = i \bmod 2$, whereas for $\alpha(i) = i \textbf{ div } 2$ each vertex has only one such neighbour. This difference explains the lower diameter and the lower average distance of $b(R(4), R(3), i \bmod 2)$ compared with those of $b(R(4), R(3), i \textbf{ div } 2)$. (End of example)

From this example we draw two conclusions. First, for $g \in G.V$ let the element $\alpha(g) \in \{0, 1\}$ be called the parity of g. Define the integer $N(\alpha)$ by

$$N(\alpha) = \mathbf{N}(h : \{g, h\} \in G.E : \alpha(g) \neq \alpha(h)).$$

Due to the α-vertex-transitivity of G, $N(\alpha)$ does not depend on g. Moreover, we have $1 \leq N(\alpha) \leq d_G$, where d_G denotes the degree of G. The upper bound is obvious. In order to prove the lower bound consider an arbitrary path in $b(G, R(m), \alpha)$ from (g, u) to (h, v) with $\alpha(g) \neq \alpha(h)$. Then the path contains two successive vertices (l, x)

and (m, y) with $\alpha(l) \neq \alpha(m)$. From $\{(l, x), (m, y)\} \in b(G, R(m), \alpha).E \wedge \alpha(l) \neq \alpha(m)$ it follows that $\{l, m\} \in G.E \wedge \alpha(l) \neq \alpha(m)$, and hence $N(\alpha) \geq 1$. Notice that when $\alpha(i) = i \ \mathbf{div} \ 2$ we have $N(\alpha) = 1$ for $G = R(4)$, and that, for $G = R(4)$ and $\alpha(i) = i \ \mathbf{mod} \ 2$, $N(\alpha) = d_G$ holds.

Second, in order to have a small bisection width it is preferable that m be even. Hereafter we therefore confine ourselves to even m. Notice that on account of corollary 3.27 we already have that $|G.V|$ is even.

Next we consider the latency and throughput of $b(G, R(m), \alpha)$. We assume that a shortest path routing algorithm is used. Hence we need to estimate the average distance of $b(G, R(m), \alpha)$. Let N and n denote the number of vertices of $b(G, R(m), \alpha)$ and G, respectively. Then we have $N = n \cdot m^2$ and $d = d_G + 2$. Following the same analysis as in the beginning of the previous section we obtain

$$B = B(G) \cdot m^2 \ \mathbf{min} \ \frac{n}{2} \cdot B(R(m)) \cdot m.$$

Hence, since $B(R(m)) = 2$ and $B \cdot W = N$, we have

$$W = \frac{n}{B(G)} \ \mathbf{max} \ m.$$

The factor $\frac{n}{2} \cdot B(R(m)) \cdot m = n \cdot m$ in the bisection width corresponds to regarding $b(G, R(m), \alpha)$ as m^2 copies of graph G with a torus-like interconnection pattern between the copies. We may also say that $b(G, R(m), \alpha)$ is a torus with multiple edges between two vertices in which each vertex has been replaced by a copy of the graph G. Formally, define the function p from $b(G, R(m), \alpha)$ to the graph H by

$p((g, u)) = u$
$\{p((g, u)), p((h, v))\} \in H.E \equiv u \neq v \ \wedge \ \{(g, u), (h, v)\} \in b(G, R(m), \alpha).E.$

Then H is isomorphic to the torus $R(m) \times R(m)$.

We therefore call the graphs $b(G, R(m), \alpha)$ the torus-connected graphs. These graphs show that with the braid operation hierarchically constructed graphs can be obtained. This hierarchical construction makes these graphs well suited for a VLSI implementation. When, for instance, a graph G can be implemented on a single chip, then a layout for $b(G, R(m), \alpha)$ can be obtained in a similar way as for a torus. Since a torus has an efficient layout with short wires, there is reason to hope that the same holds for these torus-connected graphs.

In order to calculate the average distance we first consider the diameter of $b(G, R(m), \alpha)$. Because of $A = \{0, 1\}$ and $N(\alpha) \geq 1$ and by using the same method as in the preceding section we obtain that the length of a shortest A-complete path is 1. Hence the G-part of a shortest path in $b(G, R(m), \alpha)$ from (g, u) to (h, v) is at most $1 + k_G$. Obviously, the $R(m)$-part is bounded by $2 \cdot k_{R(m)} = 2 \cdot \frac{m}{2} = m$. So we have for the diameter of $b(G, R(m), \alpha)$

$$k \leq 1 + k_G + m.$$

A lower bound is $k_G + m$, so we obtain

$$k_G + m \leq k \leq 1 + k_G + m.$$

Notice that the even parity of m has been used. When m is odd the expression becomes $k_G + 2 \cdot (m \text{ div } 2) \leq k \leq 1 + k_G + 2 \cdot (m \text{ div } 2)$. For instance, in example 3.45 we have $k = 5 = 1 + 2 + 2 \cdot (3 \text{ div } 2)$ for $b(R(4), R(3), i \text{ div } 2)$ and $k = 4 = 2 + 2 \cdot (3 \text{ div } 2)$ for $b(R(4), R(3), i \text{ mod } 2)$. On account of these formulae for the diameter we derive for the average distance $\overline{k}$ of $b(G, R(m), \alpha)$

$$\overline{k}_G + 2 \cdot \overline{k}_{R(m)} \leq \overline{k} \leq 1 + \overline{k}_G + 2 \cdot \overline{k}_{R(m)}.$$

So when m is even we have

$$\overline{k}_G + \frac{m}{2} \leq \overline{k} \leq 1 + \overline{k}_G + \frac{m}{2}.$$

We use as formula for $\overline{k}$, $\frac{1}{2} + \overline{k}_G + \frac{m}{2}$. Hence, assuming $\frac{n}{B(G)} \leq m$, the latency of $b(G, R(m), \alpha)$ is

$$T = T_e \cdot (\frac{L}{W} + \overline{k}) = T_e \cdot (\frac{L}{m} + \frac{1}{2} + \overline{k}_G + \frac{m}{2}),$$

where the edge delay T_e will be small due to the torus-like connections.

In order to estimate the throughput of $b(G, R(m), \alpha)$ the average message density per edge

$$\overline{md} = \frac{\overline{k} \cdot |b(G, R(m), \alpha).V|}{|b(G, R(m), \alpha).E|}$$

should be calculated. Since $b(G, R(m), \alpha)$ has two different types of edges, viz. G-edges and $R(m)$-edges, and message traffic differs for the two types, we treat them separately.

First we consider the average message density per G-edge. The G-part of the average distance $\overline{k}$ is $\frac{1}{2} + \overline{k}_G$, whereas the total number of G-edges in $b(G, R(m), \alpha)$ is

$$|G.E| \cdot |R(m).V|^2 = |G.E| \cdot m^2$$

on account of proposition 3.7. Hence we have

$$\overline{md}_G = \frac{(\frac{1}{2} + \overline{k}_G) \cdot n \cdot m^2}{|G.E| \cdot m^2} = (\frac{1}{2} + \overline{k}_G) \cdot n \cdot \frac{1}{|G.E|}.$$

Next the average message density per $R(m)$-edge in $b(G, R(m), \alpha)$ is calculated. Again according to proposition 3.7 the number of $R(m)$-edges in $b(G, R(m), \alpha)$ is

$$|G.V| \cdot |R(m).E| \cdot |R(m).V| = n \cdot m^2.$$

Since the $R(m)$-part of $\overline{k}$ is $\frac{m}{2}$, we have

$$\overline{md}_{R(m)} = \frac{\frac{m}{2} \cdot n \cdot m^2}{n \cdot m^2} = \frac{m}{2}.$$

So the average message density is different for the two types of edges, even when $G = R(m)$. In that case $\overline{md}_G = \frac{1}{2} + \frac{m}{4}$, and, consequently, the other $R(m)$-edges will have nearly twice as many messages on the average. Assuming $\overline{md} = \overline{md}_{R(m)}$,then by property 2.4 and $W = m$ the network capacity per vertex is $nc = 4$, which is the same value as derived in example 2.5 for k-ary n-cubes. So, when $\overline{md}_G < \overline{md}_{R(m)}$, $b(G, R(m), \alpha)$ has a higher throughput than a k-ary n-cube.

We end this section with examples of torus-connected graphs which have a low latency and a high throughput.

Example 3.48
In this example we consider the latency and throughput of 3 torus-connected graphs each with 2^{12} vertices. As in example 3.42 we assume $L = 128$ and $T_c = 1$.

The first graph is $b(R(16), R(16), i \bmod 2)$. The latency $T = \frac{L}{m} + \frac{1}{2} + \overline{k}_G + \frac{m}{2}$ is $20\frac{1}{2}$ and for $\overline{md}_G$ and $\overline{md}_{R(16)}$ we obtain $4\frac{1}{2}$ and 8, respectively. In example 3.42 we calculated the latency of this graph to be 20. The small difference is caused by the cruder estimate of $\overline{RA}$.

The next torus-connected graph we consider also appeared in example 3.42. For $b(R(4), R(32), i \bmod 2)$ we have $T = 21\frac{1}{2}, \overline{md}_G = 1\frac{1}{2}$ and $\overline{md}_{R(32)} = 16$. Notice that although $\overline{md}_{R(32)} = 2 \cdot \overline{md}_{R(16)}$ the average bit density per edge $\frac{\overline{md}}{W}$ is the same since the edges of $b(R(4), R(32), i \bmod 2)$ are twice as wide as those of $b(R(16), R(16), i \bmod 2)$. The following torus-connected graph demonstrates that applying the braid operation more than once can also give good results. Let G be the graph $b(R(4), R(2), i \bmod 2)$. Then G is the braid graph depicted in figure 3.3. G satisfies $B(G) = 4$ and $\overline{k}_G = 2\frac{1}{4}$. Define the function α from $G.V$ onto $\{0, 1\}$ by

$$\alpha((g, u)) = (g + u(0) + u(1)) \bmod 2 .$$

Then it is not difficult to verify that G is α-vertex-transitive. For $b(G, R(16), \alpha)$ the latency is $\frac{128}{16} + \frac{1}{2} + 2\frac{1}{4} + \frac{16}{2} = 18\frac{3}{4}$, while $\overline{md}_G = (\frac{1}{2} + 2\frac{1}{4}) \cdot \frac{16}{24} \simeq 2$. Hence this last graph has the lowest latency, whereas due to the wide edges the throughput of $b(R(4), R(32), i \bmod 2)$ is the highest. Since $b(R(4), R(32), i \bmod 2)$ also has an efficient layout with short wires, it may be considered as the best.

From these three braid graphs we conclude that by applying the braid operation graphs with a low latency and with a high throughput can be constructed.
(End of example)

This concludes our discussion of the braid operation.

Chapter 4

Homogeneous mappings

In this chapter we discuss some theoretical aspects of the implementation of distributed algorithms on processor networks. As argued in Chapter 1 both the algorithm and the processor network can be viewed as graphs. The algorithm is regarded as a possibly varying graph, called the computation graph, in which the vertices are processes and the edges are channels. The fixed graph corresponding to the processor network is called the implementation graph, in which the vertices are the processors and the edges are the links. Due to these abstractions an implementation of an algorithm on a processor network may be viewed as a mapping between two graphs. In the first section we introduce the notion of a homogeneous mapping, together with two simple measures of the cost of such mappings. Then we describe and analyse a method by which homogeneous mappings can be obtained. In fact, it is shown that the mapping problem for distributed algorithms in which the number of processes exceeds the number of processors is equivalent to the conventional mapping problem. Hence our approach is validated by it.

In this chapter both the computation and the implementation graph are arbitrary connected graphs. In Chapter 5 low-cost mappings of binary trees on certain processor networks are considered, whilst Chapter 6 is devoted to mappings of algorithms on braid graphs.

4.1 Homogeneous mappings and their costs

Let G be a computation graph and R be an implementation graph. An implementation of G on R has at least two objectives. A first objective is to distribute processes over processors, hence to map the vertices of G onto the vertices of R. A second objective is to map two communicating processes onto processors that are not too far apart, hence to map an edge of G onto a short path in R. We therefore define

A mapping f of G on R is a 2-tuple $< f_0, f_1 >$ such that

(i) f_0 is a function from $G.V$ to $R.V$, and

(ii) $\forall (g, h : \{g, h\} \in G.E : f_1(\{g, h\}) = shp(R, f_0(g), f_0(h)))$ where, for $r, s \in R.V$, $shp(R, r, s)$ denotes a non-empty subset of shortest paths in R from r to s.

Our main interest in mappings of G on R will be the function f_0. As far as the second component f_1 is concerned, we will only use the length of the shortest paths. How to establish these paths is determined by a routing algorithm for R, and is the topic of Chapter 7. Since routing algorithms can be non-deterministic, the subsets of shortest paths may contain more than one element. Instead of using the 2-tuple $< f_0, f_1 >$ for a mapping f of G on R we will simply write $f : G \to R$, meaning f is a mapping from G to R.

Notice that no relation between the number of vertices of G and R is assumed. This directly reflects our approach in separating the design of an algorithm from its implementation on a processor network. In many other approaches it is assumed that $|G.V| \leq |R.V|$, and attention is restricted to so-called *graph embeddings* in which each vertex of G is mapped onto a unique vertex of R (see [Ho 87, Prep81, Prep84, Rose84]). Graph embeddings, thus, form a special case of our mappings, and some notions and results for graph embeddings can be generalized for our mappings.

Next we consider which restrictions are to be imposed upon a mapping. Following the motivation of Chapter 1 we are interested in algorithms consisting of a large number of identical processes arranged in a regular structure. Hence in order to keep processors usefully busy we require that in a mapping processes are evenly distributed over the processors.

For a mapping $f : G \to R$ we denote the *number of processes mapped onto* r, $r \in R.V$, by $N(r)$:

$$N(r) = \mathbf{N}(g : g \in G.V : f(g) = r).$$

Let $p(f)$ and $q(f)$ denote the *minimum* and *maximum* number of processes that are mapped onto a processor, respectively,

$$p(f) = \mathbf{MIN}\ (r : r \in R.V : N(r))\ \text{and}\ q(f) = \mathbf{MAX}\ (r : r \in R.V : N(r)).$$

Then we define

A mapping $f : G \to R$ is called *homogeneous* if $q(f) - p(f) \leq 1$.

Corollary 4.1

Mapping $f : G \to R$ is homogeneous

$\equiv$

$p(f) = |G.V| \ \mathbf{div} \ |R.V|$ and $q(f) = (|G.V| + |R.V| - 1) \ \mathbf{div} \ |R.V|$.

(End of corollary)

A second concern of an implementation is to map two communicating processes onto processors that are not too far apart. We adopt the following two cost measures from graph embedding theory.

The dilation *cost* of a mapping $f : G \to R$ is

$$c(f) = \mathbf{MAX} \ (g, h : \{g, h\} \in G.E : k_R(f(g), f(h))),$$

where $k_R(f(g), f(h))$ denotes the distance between $f(g)$ and $f(h)$ in R.

The *average dilation cost* of a mapping $f : G \to R$ is defined by

$$av(f) = \frac{\mathbf{S}(g, h : \{g, h\} \in G.E : k_R(f(g), f(h)))}{|G.E|}.$$

The problem we are studying is, given graphs G and R, to find a homogeneous mapping from G to R with minimal dilation cost. For the sake of convenience we will omit the word dilation. It is questionable how important a cost-minimal homogeneous mapping is. A simple homogeneous mapping of nearly minimal cost is certainly preferable to an optimal homogeneous mapping which is hard to apply. We nevertheless study the above problem for two reasons: it is a theoretically interesting problem, and searching for optimal solutions gives incisive insights into the problem and often leads to simple, near optimal solutions.

In [Fish82] mappings f from G to R with $c(f) = 1$ are called emulations. In particular, (computationally) *uniform emulations* are homogeneous mappings f from G to R satisfying $c(f) = 1$ and $|G.V|$ is a multiple of $|R.V|$. An interesting and detailed analysis of uniform emulations can be found in [Bodl86]. Again, several results obtained for emulations can be generalized for our mappings. For instance, the following property is a direct generalization of lemma 5.2.1 in [Bodl86].

Property 4.2
Let G and R be graphs. For a mapping $f : G \to R$ we have

$$c(f) \leq a \equiv \forall(g, h : g, h \in G.V : k_R(f(g), f(h)) \leq a \cdot k_G(g, h)).$$

Proof
From the fact that every edge of G is mapped onto a path of length at most a in R, the assertion follows immediately.
(End of proof and property)

The next example shows that homogeneous mappings are different from both graph embeddings and emulations.

Example 4.3
Let G be the complete binary tree with vertices $\varepsilon, 0, 1, 00, 01, 10$ and 11. Let R_0 be the boolean 2-cube and R_1 be the boolean 3-cube. G can be homogeneously mapped onto R_0 with cost 1 as is shown in figure 4.4.

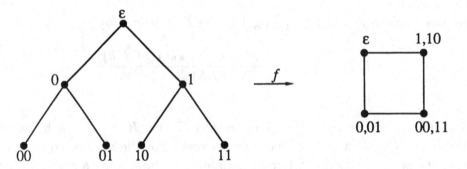

Figure 4.4: A mapping of a complete binary tree onto R_0.

But G cannot be homogeneously mapped onto R_1 with cost 1. For suppose f is a homogeneous mapping from G to R_1 with cost 1. Since $|G.V| \leq |R_1.V|$, every vertex of R_1 accommodates at most one vertex of G. Let the vertices of R_1 be identified by a sequence of three bits, such that an edge is present between two vertices that differ in one bit. Due to the vertex-transitivity of R_1 we may assume that $f(\varepsilon) = 000$. According to property 4.2 vertex 111 of R_1 cannot be the image of a vertex of G, since we have

$$\forall(h : h \in G.V : 1 \cdot k_G(\varepsilon, h) \leq 2 < 3 = k_R(f(\varepsilon), 111)).$$

The two children of ε are mapped onto two vertices of R_1 that are at distance 1 from $000 = f(\varepsilon)$. Hence the remaining vertex of R_1 that is at distance 1 from 000

accommodates a leaf vertex, say h, of G. But then we have for h and its father g

$$1 = k_G(g, h) < 2 = k_{R_1}(f(g), f(h)),$$

which according to property 4.2 contradicts $c(f) \leq 1$. In figure 4.5 one of the possible scenarios is depicted.

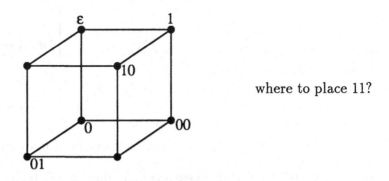

where to place 11?

Figure 4.5: A mapping of a complete binary tree onto R_1.

So, although R_1 can be uniformly emulated on R_0, embeddings of G in R_1 differ from mappings of G on R_0.
(End of example)

From example 4.3 we also conclude that with respect to cost it is advantageous to let G have more vertices than R. In the next section we show how to combine graph embeddings and uniform emulations in order to obtain homogeneous mappings.

4.2 A mapping method

In the previous section the notions of homogeneous mapping and the costs of such mappings were introduced. We now discuss a method by which homogeneous mappings can be obtained. In essence, it is proved that a homogeneous mapping is the composition of a graph embedding and a uniform emulation.

We start with an example.

Example 4.6
Let G be a graph with n vertices and R be the complete graph $K(m)$. A homogeneous mapping f from G to R with cost 1 can be obtained as follows. First the graph G

is embedded in the graph $K(n)$ by the identity function id, and then the emulation t of $K(n)$ on $K(m)$, defined by $t(i) = i \bmod m$, for $0 \le i < n$, is applied. Hence, f may be written as $t \circ id$, where $\circ$ denotes function composition.

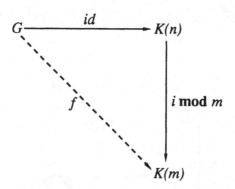

Figure 4.7: Composition of mappings

Conversely, let f be a homogeneous mapping from G to $K(m)$, and let q be $q = q(f)$, i.e., $q = \textbf{MAX}\ (r : r \in K(m).V : N(r))$, where, for $r \in K(m).V$, $N(r) = \textbf{N}(g : g \in G.V : f(g) = r)$. Then we have $\forall (r :: q - 1 \le N(r) \le q)$, since f is a homogeneous mapping. For each $r \in K(m).V$ with $N(r) = q - 1$ the processes mapped onto r can be numbered from 0 to $q - 2$. Similarly, for each $r \in K(m).V$ with $N(r) = q$ we can number the processes mapped onto it from 0 to $q - 1$. Let, for $g \in G.V$, the number that g has obtained be denoted by $nr(g)$. Then we define the embedding s of G in $K(n)$ by $s(g) = f(g) + m \cdot nr(g)$. Consequently, f is the composition of s and the above defined $t : f = t \circ s$.

Hence, when R is a complete graph, each homogeneous mapping is the composition of a graph embedding and an emulation. As we will see, we may even replace the term "emulation" in the composition by "uniform emulation".
(End of example)

Although a complete graph is an extreme example of an implementation graph, several aspects of the above example can be generalized for arbitrary graphs. In an implementation of G on R the two concerns, distributing the processes evenly over the processors and minimizing communication costs, are intermixed. By introducing an indirection via the embedding of G in a virtual processor network P, which has a similar structure to that of R, the two concerns can be separated. Notice that this also reflects our dictum of section 2.2 "the structure of the processor network should be independent of the actual number of processors". Although the introduction of P seems attractive, it also gives rise to new problems. First, instead of one mapping from G to R, two mappings, viz. one mapping from G to P and one mapping from P

to R, have to be constructed. Second, suppose G can be homogeneously mapped onto R with minimum cost a. What properties must P have to guarantee the existence of a homogeneous mapping from G to P with cost a?

Both problems can be combined by considering: Given G, R, and a homogeneous mapping $f : G \rightarrow R$ with cost a, determine a graph P that has a similar structure to that of R, an embedding $s : G \rightarrow P$, and a homogeneous mapping $t : P \rightarrow R$, such that $t \circ s = f$.

First we consider the number of vertices P should have. When $|G.V| \leq |R.V|$ we may take $P = R$. Any larger P might lead to unnecessary complications. Take, for instance, for G the complete binary tree $T(3)$ and for R the boolean 3-cube. In example 4.3 we have shown that any homogeneous mapping from $T(3)$ to the boolean 3-cube has cost at least 2. In [Wu 85] it is shown that $T(3)$ can be embedded in the boolean 4-cube with cost 1. So when we choose P equal to the boolean 4-cube, problems are shifted to the construction of the mapping t from P to the boolean 3-cube. One of the reasons for introducing P, however, is to obtain simple mappings t from P to R. We therefore choose for $|P.V|$ the smallest multiple of $|R.V|$ such that an embedding of G in P exists. According to corollary 4.1 we have $|P.V| = q \cdot |R.V|$ where q equals $(|G.V| + |R.V| - 1)$ **div** $|R.V|$.

We now turn to the composition of s and t. From the following example we conclude that the composition of two homogeneous mappings is not necessarily a homogeneous mapping.

Example 4.8
Let G be the linear array with 4 vertices and R be the linear array with three vertices. Choose for P the grid graph $P(3) \times P(2)$ (see example 3.44), and consider the following homogeneous mappings s and t. $s : G \rightarrow P$ is defined by $s(0) = (0,0), s(1) = (1,0), s(2) = (1,1)$, and $s(3) = (0,1)$, while $t : P \rightarrow R$ is given by $t(i,j) = i, 0 \leq i < 3$ and $0 \leq j < 2$. Both s and t are homogeneous mappings with cost 1. Their composition is not a homogeneous mapping, for $\mathbf{N}(g : g \in G.V : (t \circ s)(g) = 2) = 0$ whilst $\mathbf{N}(g : g \in G.V : (t \circ s)(g) = 0) = 2$.

Hence for embeddings s of G in P we have to ensure that no two "empty" vertices of P are mapped onto the same vertex of R.
(End of example)

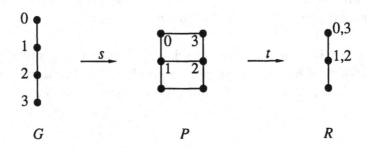

Figure 4.9: A nonhomogeneous mapping

Proposition 4.10

Let G, P, and R be graphs such that $|G.V| \leq |P.V| \wedge |P.V| = q \cdot |R.V|$, where $q = (|G.V| + |R.V| - 1) \, \mathbf{div} \, |R.V|$, and let s and t be homogeneous mappings from G to P and from P to R with costs a and b, respectively. Then we have

$$\forall(r : r \in R.V : \mathbf{N}(p : p \notin s(G) : t(p) = r) \leq 1)$$

$$\equiv$$

$t \circ s$ is a homogeneous mapping from G to R

where, for $p \in P.V$, $p \notin s(G) \equiv \forall(g : g \in G.V : s(g) \neq p)$, and $c(t \circ s) \leq a \cdot b$.

Proof

To prove the homogeneity of $t \circ s$ it is necessary and sufficient to show that $\forall(r : r \in R.V : q - 1 \leq N(r) \leq q)$ holds, where $N(r) = \mathbf{N}(g : g \in G.V : (t \circ s)(g) = r)$. Let r be an element of $R.V$. Then we have

$\quad \mathbf{N}(p : p \notin s(G) : t(p) = r) \leq 1$
$= \quad$ { calculus }
$\quad q - 1 \leq q - \mathbf{N}(p : p \notin s(G) : t(p) = r) \leq q$
$= \quad$ { t is homogeneous, $|P.V| = q \cdot |R.V|$ }
$\quad q - 1 \leq \mathbf{N}(p : p \in P.V : t(p) = r) - \mathbf{N}(p : p \notin s(G) : t(p) = r) \leq q$
$= \quad$ { s is an embedding }
$\quad q - 1 \leq \mathbf{N}(g : g \in G.V : \exists(p : p \in P.V : s(g) = p \wedge t(p) = r)) \leq q$
$= \quad$ { calculus }
$\quad q - 1 \leq \mathbf{N}(g : g \in G.V : (t \circ s)(g) = r) \leq q$
$= \quad$ { def. of $N(r)$ }
$\quad q - 1 \leq N(r) \leq q.$

From

$$\forall(g, h : g, h \in G.V : k_R((t \circ s)(g), (t \circ s)(h)) \le a \cdot b \cdot k_G(g, h))$$
$\Leftarrow \quad \{ c(s) = a, \text{ property 4.2 } \}$
$$\forall(g, h : g, h \in G.V : k_R((t \circ s)(g), (t \circ s)(h)) \le b \cdot k_P(s(g), s(h)))$$
$\Leftarrow \quad \{ c(t) = b, \text{ property 4.2 } \}$
$$\forall(g, h : g, h \in G.V : k_R((t \circ s)(g), (t \circ s)(h)) = k_R((t \circ s)(g), (t \circ s)(h)))$$
$=$

true

and property 4.2 again, it follows that $c(t \circ s) \le a \cdot b$.
(End of proof and proposition)

Hence when t is a homogeneous mapping from P to R with cost 1, i.e., t is a uniform emulation of P on R, then the composition of t and any embedding s of G in P, satisfying $\forall(r : r \in R.V : N(p : p \notin s(G) : t(p) = r) \le 1)$, yields a homogeneous mapping from G to R with cost $c(s)$. We therefore restrict attention to graphs P such that P can be uniformly emulated on R and $|P.V| = q \cdot |R.V|$. The following proposition indicates that this requirement is not too restrictive.

Proposition 4.11
Let Q be a graph and let t be the function from $Q \times R$ to R defined by $t(i, r) = r$, for $i \in Q.V$ and $r \in R.V$. Then t is a uniform emulation of $Q \times R$ on R.
(End of proposition)

Let f be a cost-minimal homogeneous mapping from G to R with $c(f) = a$. In order to obtain a composition mapping $t \circ s$ with $c(t \circ s) = a$ it is not sufficient to let P be a cartesian product graph $Q \times R$. Consider, for instance, the graphs G and R_0 of example 4.3. Then we have $a = 1$ and $q = 2$. Assuming P to be connected, Q can only be the complete graph in two vertices. Hence, $P = K(2) \times R_0$ is exactly the graph R_1 of example 4.3. But, in the same example it has been shown that the minimum cost of mapping G homogeneously on R_1 is at least 2. So, for $P = R_1$ any composition mapping $t \circ s$ has cost at least 2. Hence $Q \times R$ does not in general suffice as virtual processor network P.

Next we show that the normal product of Q and R does suffice.

The *normal product* of graphs Q and R (see [Berg73]) is the graph $Q \bullet R$ with

$$(Q \bullet R).V = Q.V \times R.V,$$

and

$$\{(q_0, r_0), (q_1, r_1)\} \in (Q \bullet R).E$$

$$\equiv$$

$$(q_0 = q_1 \wedge \{r_0, r_1\} \in R.E) \vee (\{q_0, q_1\} \in Q.E \wedge r_0 = r_1)$$
$$\vee (\{q_0, q_1\} \in Q.E \wedge \{r_0, r_1\} \in R.E).$$

Example 4.12

Let Q and R be the linear array graphs $P(2)$ and $P(3)$, respectively. The normal product graph $Q \bullet R$ is shown in figure 4.13.

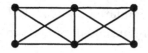

Figure 4.13: $P(2) \bullet P(3)$

(End of example)

Corresponding to proposition 4.11 we have for the normal product of R and an arbitrary graph Q

Proposition 4.14

The mapping t of $Q \bullet R$ on R, defined by $t(i, r) = r$, is a uniform emulation of $Q \bullet R$ on R.
(End of proposition)

The following theorem expresses the usefulness of the normal product operation.

Theorem 4.15
Let f be a homogeneous mapping from G to R with cost a, and let q be equal to $(|G.V| + |R.V| - 1)$ **div** $|R.V|$. Then there exist a graph Q with q vertices and a homogeneous mapping s from G to $Q \bullet R$ with cost a, such that $f = t \circ s$, where t is the mapping as defined in proposition 4.14.

Proof
As in example 4.8 we number, for each $r \in R.V$, the vertices of G that are mapped onto r from 0 through $N(r)-1$. Let for $g \in G.V$ the number assigned to g be denoted by $nr(g)$. Then we define the graph Q by

$$Q.V = \{i : 0 \le i < q : i\}, \text{ and}$$

$$\{i, j\} \in Q.E \equiv i \ne j \wedge \exists(g, h : \{g, h\} \in G.E : i = nr(g) \wedge j = nr(h)).$$

The function s from G to $Q \bullet R$ given by

$$s(g) = (nr(g), f(g))$$

is a homogeneous mapping with cost a. To verify this assertion notice that

(i) s is an embedding of G in $Q \bullet R$,

(ii)   for all $(q_0, r_0), (q_1, r_1) \in (Q \bullet R).V$

$$k((q_0, r_0), (q_1, r_1)) = k_Q(q_0, q_1) \text{ max } k_R(r_0, r_1), \text{ and}$$

(iii)   for all $g, h \in G.V$, with $\{g, h\} \in G.E$, $k_Q(nr(g), nr(h)) \le 1$.

Using property 4.2 and the definition of the cost of a mapping the assertion can be obtained.
(End of proof and theorem)

From theorem 4.15 and proposition 4.14 it follows that every homogeneous mapping is the composition of an embedding and a uniform emulation. Conversely, in the same vein as proposition 4.10, if s is an embedding of G in $Q \bullet R$, such that $|Q.V| = q, c(s) = a$, and $\forall(r : r \in R.V : N(q_0 : q_0 \in Q.V : (q_0, r) \notin s(G)) \le 1)$, then G can be homogeneously mapped on R with cost a.

This theorem shows that from a mapping point of view no extra difficulties are introduced when algorithms are considered in which the number of processes is larger than the number of processors.

Next we define a partial ordering on graphs. It is denoted by $\subseteq$ and it is, for graphs Q_0 and Q_1, defined by

$$Q_0 \subseteq Q_1 \equiv Q_0.V = Q_1.V \land Q_0.E \subseteq Q_1.E.$$

Let $G \xrightarrow{a} R$ denote that G can be homogeneously mapped on R with cost a. Then, from the definitions of a homogeneous mapping and its cost it follows that:

Property 4.16
If $Q_0 \subseteq Q_1$, then we have $G \xrightarrow{a} Q_0 \Rightarrow G \xrightarrow{a} Q_1$.
(End of property)

In particular, since the unary normal product operation $\bullet R$ is monotonic, i.e. ,

$$Q_0 \subseteq Q_1 \Rightarrow Q_0 \bullet R \subseteq Q_1 \bullet R,$$

we have that

$$Q_0 \subseteq Q_1 \Rightarrow (G \xrightarrow{a} Q_0 \bullet R \Rightarrow G \xrightarrow{a} Q_1 \bullet R)$$

holds. Hence, we may always choose for Q in theorem 4.15 the complete graph $K(q)$. In general, however, it is more interesting to search for the smallest Q, with respect to the partial ordering, that satisfies $G \xrightarrow{a} Q \bullet R$, since $|Q.E|$ indicates how many edges of G share an edge of R.

We end our analysis with two properties that will be used in the next chapter.

Property 4.17
For all graphs P, Q and R we have

(i) $P \bullet Q \simeq Q \bullet P$,

(ii) $(P \bullet Q) \bullet R \simeq P \bullet (Q \bullet R)$,

where $\simeq$ denotes "is graph isomorphic to".

Proof
See [Berg73].
(End of proof and property)

Property 4.17 states that the normal product operation is symmetric and associative. The next property is a strengthening of property 4.16.

Property 4.18
For all graphs P, Q and R we have

$$P \xrightarrow{a} R \Rightarrow P \bullet Q \xrightarrow{a} R \bullet Q.$$

Proof
Let f be a homogeneous mapping from P to R with cost a. Define the function f'
from $P \bullet Q$ to $R \bullet Q$ by

$$f'(i,j) = (f(i), j)$$

where $i \in P.V$ and $j \in Q.V$. Then f' is a homogeneous mapping with cost a.
(End of proof and property)

This concludes our discussion of homogeneous mappings in general. In the next
chapter we will apply the results obtained here to certain graphs G and R, and we
show that it can indeed be profitable that $|G.V| > |R.V|$, i.e., the number of processes
might be larger than the number of processors.

Chapter 5

Mappings of binary tree computation graphs

As described in Chapter 1 we are interested in algorithms consisting of a large collection of processes that are arranged as a regular structure. One method of obtaining such algorithms is to apply the well-known divide-and-conquer technique. The dynamic computation graph corresponding to a divide-and-conquer algorithm is a binary tree whose shape and size are determined by the problem. How to map binary trees onto certain processor networks is the subject of this chapter. Upon such mappings we impose two restrictions. First, we require that the mapping be homogeneous for a complete binary tree of any size. Moreover, in many applications the storage and time requirements differ between tree nodes of distinct heights and are the same for tree nodes of equal heights. A second requirement is, therefore, that the mapping be height-homogeneous for a complete binary tree of any size, i.e., for each height, the number of nodes of that height mapped onto a vertex of the implementation graph differs by at most one for any two vertices. Two classes of implementation graphs are discussed, viz. Sneptrees and boolean n-cubes.

5.1 Mapping binary trees onto Sneptrees

The first class of processor networks that admit a low cost (height-)homogeneous mapping of a complete binary tree is the class of Sneptrees. A Sneptree, named after its inventor J.L.A. van de Snepscheut ([Snep81]), might be considered as the degree-regular closure of a complete binary tree in much the same way as a ring is the degree-regular closure of a linear array.

Although a Sneptree is an undirected graph, for the purposes of this discussion we assign a direction to each edge. Since a Sneptree might have multiple edges and self-loops, the definition of an undirected graph given in Chapter 1 needs some adjustments. An undirected graph G consists of a nonempty set $G.V$ of vertices and a bag $G.E$ of nonempty sets that have at most two vertices from G as elements. Next, the definition of a Sneptree is given.

An *n-level Sneptree* is a directed, complete, binary tree of $2^n - 1$ vertices, with edges directed towards the leaves, augmented with 2^n edges directed out of the leaves, such that each vertex has four incident edges, two directed in and two directed out. The root and the leaves of the underlying binary tree of a Sneptree are called the root and leaves of the Sneptree as well. Of the two outgoing edges of a vertex one is called the left edge and the other the right edge, whilst the vertex pointed to by the left (right) edge of a vertex is said to be the left (right) successor of that vertex. There are many possible ways to connect the 2^n augmented edges.

Example 5.1 In figure 5.2 an example of a three-level Sneptree is shown. Notice that both the left and right edges form a spanning cycle, and that each leaf has an incoming edge from and an outgoing edge to the same vertex.

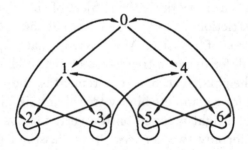

Figure 5.2: A Sneptree

(End of example)

Intermezzo 5.3
Not every degree-regular graph of degree 4 containing a complete binary tree as spanning subgraph is a Sneptree. Consider, for instance, the cartesian product graph $R(3) \times R(5)$ of a ring with three and a ring with five vertices.
In order to prove that $R(3) \times R(5)$ cannot be a Sneptree we extensively use the property of a Sneptree that only the leaves have augmented outgoing edges. Suppose $R(3) \times R(5)$ is a Sneptree. Since $R(3) \times R(5)$ is vertex-transitive we may assume that 0 is the root. As possible successors of 0 we have $1, 2, 3,$ and 12.

- Suppose 1 and 2 are the successors of 0. Then, according to the above property, an edge between 1 and 2 cannot exist.

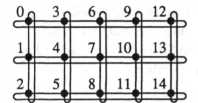 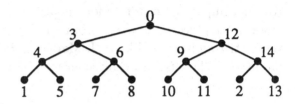

Figure 5.4: $R(3) \times R(5)$ and a spanning tree

- Suppose 1 and 3 are the successors of 0. Again, according to the above property, 2 must be a leaf. Consequently, 4 and 13 are the successors of 1, but then an edge between 3 and 4 cannot exist.

- Similarly, as in the case of 1 and 3 as successors of 0, one can prove that 2 and 3, 1 and 12, and 2 and 12 cannot be the successors of 0.

- Suppose 3 and 12 are the successors of 0. According to the above property, 4 and 5 cannot be the successors of 3. Hence, 6 is a successor of 3. Similarly, 9 must be a successor of 12. But then there cannot be an edge between 6 and 9.

Hence, $R(3) \times R(5)$ is not a Sneptree.
(End of intermezzo)

Next we concentrate upon the mapping of a binary tree onto a Sneptree. For the sake of convenience the vertices of the binary tree computation graph are called nodes. J.L.A. van de Snepscheut ([Snep81]) has shown that the mapping in which the root of the computation tree is mapped on the root of the Sneptree, and the left and right successor of a node are mapped on the left and right successor, respectively, of the vertex containing that node, is a (height-)homogeneous mapping. Obviously, this mapping has cost 1. When the computation tree is not a complete binary tree, the distribution of nodes over the vertices is strongly affected by the interconnection pattern of the Sneptree. In particular, if the binary tree is a left (right) skewed tree, i.e., a linear array, then cyclic Sneptrees give (height-)homogeneous mappings of cost 1 (see [Mart , Li 86]):

A *cyclic Sneptree* is a Sneptree with the left edges and the right edges forming two Hamiltonian cycles.

Another important criterion for Sneptrees concerns constructability. In order to generate a Sneptree recursively from smaller ones, the connection pattern should be symmetric and extensible. A.J. Martin and J.L.A. van de Snepscheut ([Mart]) have proposed a class B_n of cyclic Sneptrees fulfilling these properties.

- The two-level Sneptree B_2 is

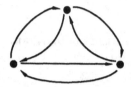

Figure 5.5: B_2

- Let C_n be the graph obtained from B_n by removing the edges (l, s) and (r, s), where s, l and r are the root, leftmost leaf, and rightmost leaf of B_n, respectively. From two instances C' and C'' of C_n the $(n + 1)$-level Sneptree B_{n+1} is constructed as shown in figure 5.6.

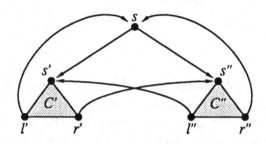

Figure 5.6: B_{n+1}

For B_{n+1}, l is identified with l' and r with r''.

The graph of example 5.1 is the Sneptree B_3. As can be proved by induction, every leaf has an incoming edge from and an outgoing edge to the same vertex. Hence there are 2^{n-2} cycles of length 2 in B_n, $n \geq 3$. Consequently, in a mapping of an unbalanced binary tree on B_n an inhomogeneous distribution of nodes over vertices might appear. In the remaining part of this section we propose another class T_n of Sneptrees, which admit a less inhomogeneous distribution of nodes over vertices for unbalanced binary trees. For $n \geq 3$, T_n has no cycles of length 2, but the other properties still hold.

We require that in constructing T_{n+1} out of two T_n's as few edges as possible should be broken. Notice that in order to have no cycles of length 2 at least six edges have to be broken in constructing a three-level Sneptree out of two two-level Sneptrees. We first give an informal description of the class T_n.

- T_2 is identical to B_2.

- Suppose $n \geq 2$. Let s, l, and r denote the root, the vertex with a left edge to the root, and the vertex with a right edge pointing to the root of T_n, respectively. Let x and y denote the leaves in T_n with a left edge of x pointing to l and with a right edge of y pointing to r. Let U' be the graph obtained from T_n by removing the edges (l,s), (r,s), and (x,l). Let U'' be the graph obtained from T_n by removing the edges (l,s), (r,s), and (y,r). Then T_{n+1} is constructed as shown in figure 5.7.

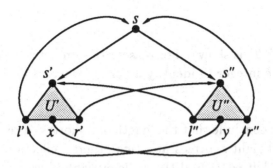

Figure 5.7: T_{n+1}

For T_{n+1}, we identify l with l' and r with r''.

The undirected version of Sneptree T_3 is the graph of example 3.18. Next a formal definition of T_n is given. For the moment we do not distinguish between the left and right edges.

The vertex set $T_n.V$ is $\{u : 1 \leq u < 2^n : u\}$, while for vertex u of T_n the outgoing edges are given by

- $(u, u - 2^{k-1})$ and $(u, u + 2^{k-1})$, for $u \bmod 2^{k+1} = 2^k$, $1 \leq k$,
- $(u, u - 1 + 2^k)$ and $(u, u + 2)$, for $u \bmod 2^{k+1} = 2^{k-1} + 1$, $2 \leq k$,
- $(u, u - 1 - 2^k)$ and $(u, u + 2)$, for $u \bmod 2^{k+1} = 2^k + 2^{k-1} + 1$, $2 \leq k$,
- $(1, 2^{n-1})$ and $(1, 3)$,

where addition (and subtraction) are assumed to be performed modulo 2^n. By considering the binary representation of a positive integer it follows that each vertex also has exactly two incoming edges. T_n contains the directed, complete, binary tree of $2^n - 1$ vertices described by the edges $(u, u - 2^{k-1})$ and $(u, u + 2^{k-1})$, for $u \bmod 2^{k+1} = 2^k, 1 \leq k$. Hence, T_n is a Sneptree with the vertex 2^{n-1} as root.

Observe that by the definition of T_n (and T_{n+1}) we have three edges in T_n that do not appear in T_{n+1}, namely $(1, 2^{n-1}), (2^{n-1} + 1, 1)$, and $(2^n - 1, 1)$. Consequently, the above defined vertices l, r, and x are the vertices $1, 2^{n-1} + 1$, and $2^n - 1$, respectively.

The graphs T_n have several interesting properties. For instance, the leaves, i.e., the vertices with an odd number, form a (directed) cycle of length 2^{n-1}, described by the edges $(u, u + 2)$. Before presenting two other properties we give an example.

Example 5.8
In figure 5.9 the graph T_4 is shown. For reasons of symmetry we use the binary representation of a positive integer to identify a vertex, whereas a left edge is represented by a dashed line.

From this drawing we conclude that the length of a shortest directed cycle is 4. Notice also that the left and right subtrees are each others' reflections, and that the same holds for the cycle of left edges and the cycle of right edges.
(End of example)

In the following property a structural resemblance between T_n and T_{n+1} is described. Let for $n \geq 2$ the mapping $p_{n+1} : T_{n+1} \to T_n$ be defined by $p_{n+1}(u) = u \bmod 2^n$, for $u \neq 2^n$, and $p_{n+1}(2^n) = 2^{n-1}$.

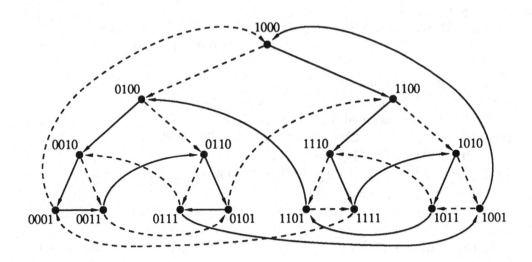

Figure 5.9: T_4

Property 5.10
p_{n+1} is a homogeneous mapping of T_{n+1} on T_n with cost 1.
(End of property)

In example 5.8 the symmetry between the left and right subtrees of T_4 was mentioned. This symmetry is a direct consequence of

Property 5.11
The mapping $q_n : T_n \to T_n$, defined by

$$q_n(2^{n-1}) = 2^{n-1} \text{ and } q_n(u) = (u + 2^{n-1}) \bmod 2^n, \text{ for } u \neq 2^{n-1},$$

is an automorphism of T_n, i.e., q_n is a one-to-one mapping from $T_n.V$ to $T_n.V$, and, for all $u, v \in T_n.V, q_n$ satisfies

$$(u, v) \in T_n.E \equiv (q_n(u), q_n(v)) \in T_n.E.$$

Proof
It is clear that q_n is a one-to-one mapping. From the definition of the edge set of T_n we conclude that four cases have to be distinguished. Of these four only one case is considered; the other three can be treated similarly.

$(u, v) \in T_n.E \wedge u \bmod 2^{k+1} = 2^k \wedge 1 \le k$

$=$ $\{\, 1 \le u < 2^n \,\}$
$(v = u - 2^{k-1} \vee v = u + 2^{k-1}) \wedge ((u \bmod 2^{k+1} = 2^k \wedge 1 \le k < n - 1)$
$\qquad\qquad\qquad\qquad\qquad \vee (u = 2^{n-1} \wedge k = n - 1))$

$=$

$((v = u - 2^{k-1} \vee v = u + 2^{k-1}) \wedge u \bmod 2^{k+1} = 2^k \wedge 1 \le k < n - 1)\ \vee$
$((v = 2^{n-1} - 2^{n-2} \vee v = 2^{n-1} + 2^{n-2}) \wedge u = 2^{n-1} \wedge k = n - 1)$

$=$ $\{\text{ addition is performed modulo } 2^n \text{ in } T_n \,\}$
$((v + 2^{n-1} = u + 2^{n-1} - 2^{k-1} \vee v + 2^{n-1} = u + 2^{n-1} + 2^{k-1})$
$\quad \wedge u \bmod 2^{k+1} = 2^k \wedge 1 \le k < n - 1)$
$\vee((v + 2^{n-1} = 2^{n-1} + 2^{n-2} \vee v + 2^{n-1} = 2^{n-2}) \wedge u = 2^{n-1} \wedge k = n - 1)$

$=$ $\{\text{ definition of } q_n, v \ne 2^{n-1} \,\}$
$((q_n(v) = q_n(u) - 2^{k-1} \vee q_n(v) = q_n(u) + 2^{k-1}) \wedge q_n(u) \bmod 2^{k+1} = 2^k$
$\qquad\qquad\qquad\qquad\qquad\qquad\qquad \wedge 1 \le k < n - 1)$
$\vee((q_n(v) = q_n(u) + 2^{n-2} \vee q_n(v) = q_n(u) - 2^{n-2}) \wedge q_n(u) = 2^{n-1} \wedge k = n - 1)$

$=$

$(q_n(u), q_n(v)) \in T_n.E \wedge q_n(u) \bmod 2^{k+1} = 2^k \wedge 1 \le k.$

(End of proof and property)

As we have seen, when a linear array is mapped onto a Sneptree, then cyclic Sneptrees give minimal cost (height-)homogeneous mappings.

Property 5.12
T_n is cyclic.

Proof
We use induction on n to prove that T_n has a Hamiltonian cycle of left edges and a Hamiltonian cycle of right edges.
T_2 is cyclic, since it has the two edge-disjoint Hamiltonian cycles $< 2, 1, 3, 2 >$ and $< 2, 3, 1, 2 >$.
Let P be the property that $T_n, n \ge 3$, has two edge-disjoint Hamiltonian cycles L_n and R_n of the form

$L_n\ =\ < 2^{n-1}, A, 2, 3, B, 2^n - 1, 1, 2^{n-1} >,$
$R_n\ =\ < 2^{n-1}, C, 2, 1, 3, D, 2^{n-1} + 1, 2^{n-1} >,$

such that $R_n = q_n(L_n)$, where q_n is the mapping defined in property 5.11, and $A, B, C,$ and D denote paths in T_n.

- $n = 3$.

  Since T_3 contains the cycles $< 4, 2, 3, 6, 5, 7, 1, 4 >$ and $< 4, 6, 7, 2, 1, 3, 5, 4 >$, T_3 fulfils P.

- $n \geq 3$.

  Let T_n satisfy the property P. Consider the cycle L_n. L_n contains two edges of T_n that are not present in T_{n+1}, viz. $(2^n - 1, 1)$ and $(1, 2^{n-1})$. Hence by removing those edges of L_n and by noticing that T_n always contains the edges $(2, 1)$ and $(1, 3)$, a path L'_n of T_n is obtained, whose edges also appear in T_{n+1}:

  $$L'_n =< 2^{n-1}, A, 2, 1, 3, B, 2^n - 1 > .$$

  Next, by applying the automorphism q_{n+1} of T_{n+1} on L'_n we obtain a path $q_{n+1}(L'_n)$ of T_{n+1} which visits each vertex u of T_{n+1} satisfying $2^n < u < 2^{n+1}$:

  $$q_{n+1}(L'_n) =< 2^n + 2^{n-1}, q_{n+1}(A), 2^n + 2, 2^n + 1, 2^n + 3, q_{n+1}(B), 2^{n+1} - 1 > .$$

  Regarding the cycle R_n of T_n, only the edge $(2^{n-1} + 1, 2^{n-1})$ does not appear in T_{n+1}. Consequently, by removing this edge and the edges $(2, 1)$ and $(1, 3)$, and by adding edge $(2, 3)$ we obtain a path R'_n of T_{n+1} which visits each vertex u of T_{n+1} satisfying $1 < u < 2^n$:

  $$R'_n =< 2^{n-1}, C, 2, 3, D, 2^{n-1} + 1 > .$$

  By noticing that T_{n+1} has the edges $(2^n, 2^{n-1}), (2^{n-1} + 1, 2^n + 2^{n-1}), (2^{n+1} - 1, 1)$, and $(1, 2^n)$, we define the Hamiltonian cycle L_{n+1} as

  $$L_{n+1} =< 2^n, R'_n, q_{n+1}(L'_n), 1, 2^n > .$$

  The other Hamiltonian cycle R_{n+1} is simply defined by $R_{n+1} = q_{n+1}(L_{n+1})$. Hence, since $q_{n+1} \circ q_{n+1} = id$, we have

  $$R_{n+1} =< 2^n, q_{n+1}(R'_n), L'_n, 2^n + 1, 2^n > .$$

  So L_{n+1} and R_{n+1} have the required form. From the fact that L'_n and R'_n are edge-disjoint and q_{n+1} is an automorphism, it follows that L_{n+1} and R_{n+1} are also edge-disjoint. Hence, T_{n+1} satisfies property P.

(End of proof and property)

To resume, from the definition and properties 5.10-5.12 we conclude that T_n is extensible, symmetric, and cyclic. According to example 5.8 the length of a shortest directed cycle in T_4 is 4, so, for $n \geq 4$, T_n has by construction no cycles of length less than 4. Since these cycles of length 4 also appear in $B_n, n \geq 4$, and B_n has cycles of length 2, we infer that, in general, T_n admits less inhomogeneous mappings than B_n. There are, however, many other interconnection patterns for Sneptrees. We have introduced the class T_n only as an alternative to the class B_n and as an experiment with Sneptrees. Nevertheless, the results obtained for T_n will be used in the next section for mappings of binary trees onto boolean n-cubes.

5.2 Mappings of binary trees onto boolean n-cubes

Boolean n-cubes form a second class of processor networks, which admit low cost (height-)homogeneous mappings of complete binary trees of any size. In effect, we will show by construction the existence of cost-minimal mappings of cost 2 for a boolean n-cube.

First we give some notational conventions. As usual, a vertex u of a boolean n-cube, denoted by $BC(n)$, is identified by a sequence $u(i : 0 \leq i < n)$ of bits. Two vertices, u and v say, are adjacent if $\mathbf{N}(i : 0 \leq i < n : u(i) \neq v(i)) = 1$. In order to distinguish between the nodes of a binary tree and the vertices of a boolean n-cube we use the following notation for binary trees. A binary tree is an undirected graph BT with vertex set $BT.V$ and edge set $BT.E$ such that $BT.V$ is a prefix-closed subset of $\{a, b\}^*$, and

$$\forall (x, y : x, y \in BT.V \land (y = xa \lor y = xb) : \{x, y\} \in BT.E).$$

Let $BT(k)$ denote a complete binary tree with $2^k - 1$ vertices. In the literature we have found the following results concerning the mapping of $BT(k)$ on boolean n-cube $BC(n)$ (see [Wu 85, Desh86]): (assuming $n \geq 3$)

$BT(k)$ can be mapped on $BC(n)$ with minimum cost 1, for $k < n$, and with minimum cost 2, for $k = n$.

Notice that in both cases the mappings are embeddings (see section 4.1), so they are (height-)homogeneous. As motivated in Chapter 1 we are especially interested in the case that the number of nodes exceeds the number of vertices, so from now on we assume $k > n$. We start with $k = n + 1$, and consider homogeneous, but not necessarily height-homogeneous, mappings of $BT(n+1)$ on $BC(n)$ first.

Although it was not described as such, we have already encountered a cost two homogeneous mapping of $BT(n+1)$ on $BC(n)$ in the previous section. Consider the definition of the complete, directed binary tree within the Sneptree T_{n+1}. It has as vertex set $\{u : 1 \le u < 2^{n+1} : u\}$ and edges $(u, u - 2^{m-1})$ and $(u, u + 2^{m-1})$ for vertex u satisfying $u \bmod 2^{m+1} = 2^m$, where $1 \le m$. Let for each $u, 0 \le u < 2^{n+1}$, the sequence $bin(u)(i : 0 \le i < n+1)$ denote the binary representation of u, i.e., $u = \mathbf{S}(i : 0 \le i < n+1 : bin(u)(i) \cdot 2^i)$. Then we have, for all u and m such that $u \bmod 2^{m+1} = 2^m \wedge 1 \le m$,

$$\forall(i : 0 \le i < m - 1 : bin(u)(i) = bin(u - 2^{m-1})(i) \wedge bin(u)(i) = bin(u + 2^{m-1})(i))$$
$$\wedge\ bin(u)(m-1) = 0 \wedge bin(u - 2^{m-1})(m-1) = 1 \wedge bin(u + 2^{m-1})(m-1) = 1$$
$$\wedge\ bin(u)(m) = 1 \wedge bin(u - 2^{m-1})(m) = 0 \wedge bin(u + 2^{m-1})(m) = 1$$
$$\wedge\ \forall(i : m + 1 \le i < n + 1 : bin(u)(i) = bin(u - 2^{m-1})(i) \wedge$$
$$bin(u)(i) = bin(u + 2^{m-1})(i)).$$

Hence, $bin(u)$ and $bin(u - 2^{m-1})$ differ in two indices, while $bin(u)$ and $bin(u + 2^{m-1})$ in just one index. Consequently by noticing that the root is vertex 2^n, the function f from $BT(n+1)$ to $BC(n+1)$ inductively defined by

- $f(\varepsilon) = bin(2^n)$,

- if, for a non-leaf node x, $f(x) = bin(u)$ with $u \bmod 2^{m+1} = 2^m, 1 \le m$, then $f(xa) = bin(u - 2^{m-1})$ and $f(xb) = bin(u + 2^{m-1})$,

is a homogeneous mapping of $BT(n+1)$ on $BC(n+1)$ with cost 2. Observe that 0 is the only "empty" vertex. So, according to proposition 4.10, in order to obtain a homogeneous mapping of $BT(n+1)$ on $BC(n)$ with cost at most 2, it remains to define a homogeneous mapping of $BC(n+1)$ on $BC(n)$ with cost 1. By virtue of property 5.10 we can, for instance, choose the function t defined by $t(y) = y \bmod 2^n$, for $0 \le y < 2^{n+1}$, thereby using the one-to-one correspondence between a natural number and its binary representation. Using the same correspondence the resulting mapping $g_0 = t \circ f$ is given by (assuming $n \ge 1$)

- $g_0(\varepsilon) = 0, g_0(a) = g_0(b) = 2^{n-1}$,

- if, for a non-leaf node x, $g_0(x) = v$ with $v \bmod 2^{m+1} = 2^m$, $1 \le m$, then $g_0(xa) = v - 2^{m-1}$ and $g_0(xb) = v + 2^{m-1}$.

Since $g_0(a) = g_0(b)$ and, for $n \ge 2$, $g_0(aa) = 2^{n-2}$, we conclude that g_0 is not height-homogeneous, and that, for $n \ge 2$, g_0 has cost 2. Notice, however, that when we choose for t the function $t(y) = y \textbf{ div } 2, 0 \leq y < 2^{n+1}$, then a height-homogeneous mapping g_1 with cost 2 is obtained, because the leaves of $BT(n+1)$ are mapped by f onto the vertices with an odd number. This mapping g_1 is given by (again assuming $n \geq 1$)

- $g_1(\varepsilon) = 2^{n-1}$,

- if, for a non-leaf node x, $g_1(x) = v \textbf{ div } 2$ with $v \textbf{ mod } 2^{m+1} = 2^m$, $1 \leq m$, then
  $g_1(xa) = (v - 2^{m-1}) \textbf{ div } 2$ and $g_1(xb) = (v + 2^{m-1}) \textbf{ div } 2$.

The construction of the height-homogeneous mapping g_1 – neither in [Wu 85] nor in [Desh86] is an algorithm explicitly given – shows the usefulness of the method described in section 4.2. The method is even applicable when $k = n$, by omitting the leaves of $BT(n+1)$. Theorem 4.15 in the same section, however, states that we may consider $BC(n) \bullet K(2)$ as a virtual processor network instead of the cartesian product $BC(n+1) = BC(n) \times K(2)$. As in example 4.3 we will show that $BT(n+1)$ can be homogeneously mapped on $BC(n)$ with cost 1, while according to [Wu 85, Desh86] a cost-minimal homogeneous mapping of $BT(n+1)$ on $BC(n+1)$ has cost 2. Notice that these results imply that it can be advantageous to let the computation graph have more vertices than the implementation graph.

As in Chapter 4 we denote the existence of a homogeneous mapping from graph G to graph R with cost c by $G \overset{c}{\rightarrow} R$. As stated above, we have

Theorem 5.13
For all n, $n \geq 0$, $BT(n+1) \overset{1}{\rightarrow} BC(n) \bullet K(2)$.

Proof
Since $BT(1)$ consists of just one node, the theorem is trivially true for $n = 0$. So suppose $n \geq 1$. In order to prove the theorem inductively we first give two embeddings of $BC(n-1) \bullet K(2)$ in $BC(n) \bullet K(2)$ with cost 1. Assume $u \in BC(n-1).V, v \in BC(n).V$, and $z \in K(2).V$.

- The mapping $id_{n-1} : BC(n-1) \bullet K(2) \rightarrow BC(n) \bullet K(2)$ is given by

$$id_{n-1}((u, z)) = (v, z),$$

such that $\forall(i : 0 \leq i < n - 1 : u(i) = v(i)) \wedge v(n-1) = 0$.

- For $n \geq 2$ we define the mapping $ex_{n-1} : BC(n-1) \bullet K(2) \to BC(n) \bullet K(2)$ by

$$ex_1((u,z)) = (v,z) \quad \text{with} \quad u(0) = v(0) \wedge v(1) = 1 \text{ , and, for } n \geq 3,$$
$$ex_{n-1}((u,z)) = (v,z) \quad \text{with} \quad \forall(i : 0 \leq i < n-3 : u(i) = v(i)) \wedge v(n-1) = 1$$
$$\wedge u(n-3) = v(n-2) \wedge u(n-2) = v(n-3).$$

Applying, for $n \geq 3$, the mapping ex_{n-1} on (u,z) can, with respect to the bit pattern of u, be interpreted as exchanging the two most significant bits of u and extending the bit pattern with a one.

On account of property 4.18 the verification that both mappings are homogeneous and have cost 1 is straightforward.

Consider a homogeneous mapping f from $BT(n+1)$ to $BC(n) \bullet K(2)$. Since $|BT(n+1).V| = |(BC(n) \bullet K(2)).V| - 1$, f leaves one vertex of $BC(n) \bullet K(2)$ "free". This vertex is denoted as $free(f)$. Next we formulate the induction hypothesis.

Let P_{n+1} be the property that $BT(n+1)$ can be homogeneously mapped on $BC(n) \bullet K(2)$ by a function f_{n+1} with $c(f_{n+1}) = 1$, satisfying

$$f_{n+1}(\varepsilon) = (bin_n(0), 0), f_{n+1}(a) = (bin_n(2^{n-1}), 0), f_{n+1}(b) = (bin_n(0), 1),$$
$$\text{and } free(f_{n+1}) = (bin_n(2^{n-1}), 1),$$

where, for $0 \leq y < 2^n$, $bin_n(y)$ denotes the binary representation of y.

- $n = 1$.

Define the mapping f_2 from $BT(2)$ to $BC(1) \bullet K(2)$ by $f_2(\varepsilon) = (0,0), f_2(a) = (1,0), f_2(b) = (0,1)$, and $free(f_2) = (1,1)$. In figure 5.14 it is shown that f_2 is homogeneous and has cost 1, so P_2 holds.

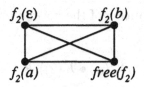

Figure 5.14: $BC(1) \bullet K(2)$

- $n > 1$.

Let f_n be a mapping from $BT(n)$ to $BC(n-1) \bullet K(2)$ such that P_n holds. Then we define $f_{n+1} : BT(n+1) \to BC(n) \bullet K(2)$ by

$f_{n+1}(\varepsilon) = (bin_n(0), 0), f_{n+1}(a) = (bin_n(2^{n-1}), 0), f_{n+1}(b) = (bin_n(0), 1),$
$free(f_{n+1}) = (bin_n(2^{n-1}), 1),$
$f_{n+1}(ab) = ex_{n-1}(free(f_n)), f_{n+1}(ba) = id_{n-1}(free(f_n)),$
$f_{n+1}(aax) = ex_{n-1}(f_n(ax)), \quad$ for $aax \in BT(n+1).V,$
$f_{n+1}(abx) = id_{n-1}(f_n(bx)), \quad$ for $x \neq \varepsilon \wedge abx \in BT(n+1).V,$
$f_{n+1}(bax) = ex_{n-1}(f_n(bx)), \quad$ for $x \neq \varepsilon \wedge bax \in BT(n+1).V,$
$f_{n+1}(bbx) = id_{n-1}(f_n(ax)), \quad$ for $bbx \in BT(n+1).V.$

From this definition it is clear that f_{n+1} has the required form, so only the homogeneity and the cost of f_{n+1} have to be verified.

We show the homogeneity of f_{n+1} by proving that f_{n+1} is an embedding. From

$\quad (v, z) \in (BC(n) \bullet K(2)).V \wedge v(n-1) = 0$
$=\quad$ { def. of id_{n-1} }
$\quad (v, z) \in id_{n-1}((BC(n-1) \bullet K(2)).V)$
$=\quad$ { ind. hyp. }
$\quad (v, z) \in id_{n-1}(f_n(BT(n).V)) \cup \{id_{n-1}(free(f_n))\}$
$=\quad$ { def. of $BT(n)$ }
$\quad (v, z) \in \{id_{n-1}(f_n(\varepsilon))\} \cup \{id_{n-1}(f_n(b))\} \cup \{id_{n-1}(free(f_n))\} \cup$
$\quad \{x : ax \in BT(n).V : id_{n-1}(f_n(ax))\} \cup$
$\quad \{x : x \neq \varepsilon \wedge bx \in BT(n).V : id_{n-1}(f_n(bx))\}$
$=\quad$ { def. of f_{n+1}, id_{n-1}, and $BT(n)$ }
$\quad (v, z) \in \{f_{n+1}(\varepsilon)\} \cup \{f_{n+1}(b)\} \cup \{x : bbx \in BT(n+1).V : f_{n+1}(bbx)\}$
$\quad\quad\quad \cup \{x : x \neq \varepsilon \wedge abx \in BT(n+1).V : f_{n+1}(abx)\} \cup \{f_{n+1}(ba)\},$

and a similar proof that

$\quad (v, z) \in (BC(n) \bullet K(2)).V \wedge v(n-1) = 1$
$\Rightarrow$
$\quad (v, z) \in f_{n+1}(BT(n+1).V) \cup \{free(f_{n+1})\},$

we conclude that f_{n+1} is indeed an embedding.

In order to prove that f_{n+1} has cost 1 we observe that

(0) according to the definition of the normal product and of a complete graph, we have

$$\{(v, y), (w, z)\} \in (BC(n) \bullet K(2)).E$$
$$\equiv$$
$$\{v, w\} \in BC(n).E \vee (v = w \wedge y \neq z),$$

(1) id_{n-1} and ex_{n-1} have cost 1,

(2) $id_{n-1} \circ f_n$ and $ex_{n-1} \circ f_n$ are embeddings, and

(3) on account of the induction hypothesis f_n has cost 1 and
$\{free(f_n), f_n(\varepsilon)\} \in (BC(n-1) \bullet K(2)).E$ holds.

From the definition of f_{n+1} and (0) it follows that $f_{n+1}(\varepsilon)$ and $f_{n+1}(a)$ are adjacent. Using (1),(2),(3), and proposition 4.10 we obtain that $id_{n-1} \circ f_n$ and $ex_{n-1} \circ f_n$ have cost 1. Hence, since $f_{n+1}(\varepsilon) = id_{n-1}(f_n(\varepsilon)), f_{n+1}(a) = ex_{n-1}(f_n(\varepsilon))$, and $f_{n+1}(b) = id_{n-1}(f_n(b))$, in order to prove that f_{n+1} has cost 1, it suffices to show that

$$\{f_{n+1}(ab), f_{n+1}(abx)\} \in (BC(n) \bullet K(2)).E, \quad \text{for } (x = a \vee x = b) \wedge n \geq 3,$$
and $\{f_{n+1}(ba), f_{n+1}(bax)\} \in (BC(n) \bullet K(2)).E, \quad \text{for } (x = a \vee x = b) \wedge n \geq 3.$

Consequently, for $n = 2$ we have obtained that P_{n+1} holds. Assume $n \geq 3$. Using induction on n it follows that

$$(4) \ f_{n+1}(ba) = (bin_n(2^{n-2}), 1) \wedge f_{n+1}(bb) = (bin_n(2^{n-2}), 0)$$

holds. Hence, we have

$\qquad \{f_{n+1}(ab), f_{n+1}(aba)\} \in (BC(n) \bullet K(2)).E$
$=\qquad \{ \text{ def. of } f_{n+1} \}$
$\qquad \{ex_{n-1}(free(f_n)), id_{n-1}(f_n(ba))\} \in (BC(n) \bullet K(2)).E$
$=\qquad \{ \text{ ind. hyp, (4) } \}$
$\qquad \{ex_{n-1}(bin_{n-1}(2^{n-2}), 1), id_{n-1}(bin_{n-1}(2^{n-3}), 1)\} \in (BC(n) \bullet K(2)).E$
$=\qquad \{ \text{ def. of } ex_{n-1} \text{ and } id_{n-1} \}$
$\qquad \{(bin_n(2^{n-1} + 2^{n-3}), 1), (bin_n(2^{n-3}), 1)\} \in (BC(n) \bullet K(2)).E$
$=\qquad \{ (0) \}$
$\qquad true.$

Since the other cases can be treated similarly, we conclude that f_{n+1} has cost 1, and, hence, P_{n+1} holds. This concludes the lengthy proof.

Notice that the resulting mapping g_{n+1} from $BT(n+1)$ to $BC(n)$ defined by $g_{n+1} = p \circ f_{n+1}$, where $p : BC(n) \bullet K(2) \to BC(n)$ is given by $p((v, z)) = v$, is not height-homogeneous. For instance we have $g_{n+1}(ab) = g_{n+1}(bb)$, for $n \geq 2$. In figure 5.15 the mappings f_3 and f_4 are illustrated. The 2-tuple in a node denotes its image under the mapping $f_i, i = 3, 4$.
(End of proof and theorem)

Combining theorem 5.13 and the results of Chapter 4 and of [Wu 85, Desh86] leads to the following remarkable corollary:

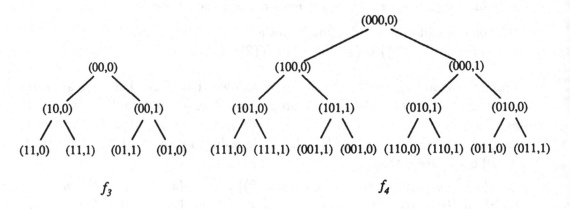

Figure 5.15: f_3 and f_4

Corollary 5.16
For $n \geq 3$ we have

the complete binary tree $BT(k)$ can be homogeneously mapped onto the boolean n-cube with cost 1, for $k \neq n$, and with minimum cost 2 for $k = n$.

Proof
For $k \leq n$, the corollary is a reformulation of the results in [Wu 85, Desh86]. So suppose $k > n$. According to theorem 5.13 we have

$$BT(k) \overset{1}{\to} BC(k-1) \bullet K(2)$$
$$\Rightarrow \quad \{ \text{ property 4.18, } BC(k-1) \overset{1}{\to} BC(n) \}$$
$$BT(k) \overset{1}{\to} BC(n) \bullet K(2)$$
$$\Rightarrow \quad \{ BC(n) \bullet K(2) \overset{1}{\to} BC(n) \}$$
$$BT(k) \overset{1}{\to} BC(n),$$

where we have used that in each case the composition of two homogeneous mapping is again a homogeneous mapping, since there is only one "empty" vertex.
(End of proof and corollary)

Consequently, in the design of algorithms for a boolean n-cube it is disadvantageous to have the number of processes determined by the size of the cube.

The mappings from a complete binary tree to a boolean n-cube considered so far do not lend themselves to generalization for dynamic, possibly incomplete, binary

trees. Moreover, as mentioned in the introduction to this chapter, we are interested
in homogeneous mappings that are also height-homogeneous. We therefore first determine the minimum cost of mapping a complete binary tree both homogeneously
and height-homogeneously on a boolean n-cube. Assume $n \geq 3$; then we have

Theorem 5.17
A cost-minimal, homogeneous, and height-homogeneous mapping from $BT(k)$ to
$BC(n)$ has cost 1 for $k < n$, and cost 2 for $k \geq n$.

Proof
Let f be a cost-minimal, homogeneous, height-homogeneous mapping from $BT(k)$
to $BC(n)$. Since for $k \leq n$ each homogeneous mapping is also height-homogeneous,
the theorem follows in that case from corollary 5.16. So suppose $k > n$, and consider
a height h, satisfying $n \leq h < k$. $BT(k)$ has 2^h nodes of height h. So due to the
height-homogeneity of f, the number of nodes of height h mapped onto a vertex of
$BC(n)$ is 2^{h-n}. Hence, $\mathbf{S}(h : n \leq h < k : 2^{h-n}) = 2^{k-n} - 1$ nodes of height at least
n are mapped onto a vertex. Since, by the homogeneity of f, each vertex has to
accommodate either $2^{k-n} - 1$ or 2^{k-n} nodes, the number of nodes of height less than
n mapped onto a vertex is at most 1. Restricting f to the nodes of height less than
n results, thus, in a homogeneous mapping from $BT(n)$ to $BC(n)$. So, on account of
corollary 5.16, f has cost at least 2. In order to show that cost 2 can be achieved, we
use the homogeneous and height-homogeneous mapping g_1 from $BT(n+1)$ to $BC(n)$
that was defined in the beginning of this section. Due to the height-homogeneity of g_1,
each vertex is the image of exactly one leaf of $BT(n+1)$. Hence, by mapping the two
successors of a node x of height $h, n \leq h < k-1$, onto $g_1(x)$, a (height-)homogeneous
mapping g from $BT(k)$ to $BC(n)$ is obtained. Formally, g can be defined by

$$-g(y) = g_1(y), \quad \text{for } y \in BT(n+1),$$
$$-g(yz) = g_1(y), \quad \text{for } y \in BT(n+1) \wedge yz \in BT(k).$$

Obviously, g has the same cost as g_1. Hence, $BT(k)$ can be homogeneously and
height-homogeneously mapped onto $BC(n)$ with cost 2.
(End of proof and theorem)

Although the above defined g has minimum cost and can be used for arbitrary trees,
we do not consider g a suitable mapping. When g is applied to incomplete binary
trees, a very inhomogeneous distribution of nodes over vertices might appear. Instead
of g we therefore present a mapping f, which also has cost 2, but which admits a
more uniform distribution of nodes over vertices when incomplete binary trees are
considered.

Before describing f, we first consider what properties f should have besides the homogeneity and height-homogeneity for complete binary trees.

First, in order to keep f as simple as possible, when a node has been mapped onto a vertex, it should remain on that vertex. Or, in standard terminology f must be static.

Second, in order to avoid an inhomogeneous distribution of nodes over vertices in the case of incomplete binary trees, a successor of a node should be mapped onto a vertex differing from the vertex on which the node has been mapped. Moreover, if a node has two successors, then these two successors should be mapped onto distinct vertices.

Third, for the same reason as above, when two nodes of different height are mapped onto the same vertex, then their successors should be mapped onto vertices as different as possible.

Notice, however, that these requirements are not that definite. We certainly prefer a simple mapping that partly fulfils these requirements, to a complicated mapping that perfectly suits them.

Next we give a kind of "derivation" of f, proceeding as if the tree on which f has to be applied is growing in such a way that each time it is a complete binary tree.

In order for a complete binary tree of less than 2^n nodes to be homogeneous, the nodes of height less than n have to be mapped onto distinct vertices. Let h be an integer satisfying $0 \le h < n$. There are 2^h nodes of height h in a complete binary tree. Since there are also exactly 2^h vertices u in a boolean n-cube that satisfy

$$\forall(i : h < i < n : u(i) = 0) \wedge u(h) = 1,$$

it seems natural to map the nodes of height h onto those 2^h vertices. Doing so leads to $f(\varepsilon) = 0\cdots001$, $f(a) = 0\cdots011$, and $f(b) = 0\cdots010$, where we have used the symmetry in the left and right successors of a node. Hence, bit pattern $0\cdots001y$ of $f(x)$ is changed into bit pattern $0\cdots011y$ for the left successor and into $0\cdots010y$ for the right successor. We choose to keep this invariant for each node of height $l, 0 \le l < n - 1$. So, if x is a node of height $m - 1, 0 \le m - 1 < n - 1$, then $f(xa) = c_m(f(x))$ and $f(xb) = (c_m \circ c_{m-1})(f(x))$, where, for $0 \le i < n$, c_i denotes the mapping by which the ith bit is complemented, i.e., for $u, v \in BC(n).V$,

$$c_i(u) = v \text{ such that } \forall(j : 0 \le j < n \wedge j \ne i : u(j) = v(j)) \wedge u(i) \ne v(i).$$

Applying this scheme results in a (height-)homogeneous mapping f from $BT(n)$ to $BC(n)$ with cost 2, such that the nodes of height $(n-1)$, i.e., the leaves of $BT(n)$, are mapped onto the vertices u satisfying $u(n-1) = 1$. When the tree grows, then by convention all the leaves get two successors. Hence we obtain 2^n nodes of height n. So in order to be homogeneous for height n, f has to establish a one-to-one mapping between the nodes of height n and the vertices of $BC(n)$. Considering the above invariant, a node of height less than $n-1$ and its left successor are mapped onto vertices that differ in one bit position, say p, while its right successor's vertex differs in position p and one other bit position, say q, from the vertex onto which the node is mapped. So, in order to obtain the same mapping scheme for any height, we may express the mapping of the height n nodes as follows. For node x, let $ht(x)$ denote the height of x. Then we require a p and q, $0 \le p < n-1 \land 0 \le q < n \land p \ne q$, such that for each node x with $ht(x) = n-1$ we have

$$f(xa) = c_p(f(x)) \text{ and } f(xb) = (c_p \circ c_q)(f(x)), \text{ and}$$
$$\{x : ht(x) = n-1 : c_p(f(x))\} \cup \{x : ht(x) = n-1 : (c_p \circ c_q)(f(x))\} = BC(n).V.$$

Let x be a node with $ht(x) = n-1$, and assume $u = f(x)$. Then we have $u(n-1) = 1$, according to the invariant. Hence, in order to obtain all vertices of $BC(n)$, it is necessary and sufficient to require that $0 \le p < n-1 \land q = n-1$ holds.

Recapitulating all we have derived so far, we have the following scheme for the mapping f restricted to nodes of height at most n:

$$f(\varepsilon) \quad = 0 \cdots 01,$$
$$f(xa) \quad = c_p(f(x)), f(xb) = (c_p \circ c_q)(f(x)),$$
$$\qquad \text{for } 1 \le ht(xa) < n, \text{ where } p = ht(xa) \land q = p-1 = ht(x),$$
$$f(xa) \quad = c_p(f(x)), f(xb) = (c_p \circ c_q)(f(x)),$$
$$\qquad \text{for } 1 \le ht(xa) = n, \text{ where } 0 \le p < n-1 \land q = n-1 = ht(x).$$

Next we give a generalization of this scheme such that it can also be applied for nodes of height greater than n. Let $s(i : i \ge 0)$ be an infinite sequence of elements of $\{j : 0 \le j < n\}$ that satisfies $\forall(i : 0 \le i < n : s(i) = i)$. Then we define f by

$$f(\varepsilon) \quad = 0 \cdots 01,$$
$$f(xa) \quad = c_{s(i)}(f(x)), \qquad \text{where } i = ht(xa), \text{ and}$$
$$f(xb) \quad = (c_{s(i)} \circ c_{s(i-1)})(f(x)), \quad \text{where } i = ht(xb).$$

Obviously, the scheme defined above for nodes of height at most n fits within this definition. So f is (height-)homogeneous for complete binary trees with at most $2^{n+1}-1$ nodes. To conclude that f is also (height-)homogeneous for larger, complete, binary trees, notice that both c_l and $c_l \circ c_m$ are automorphisms of $BC(n)$, for $0 \leq l, m < n$. Hence f is a homogeneous and height-homogeneous mapping for complete, binary trees of any size.

Next we consider the three requirements that we formulated just before the derivation of f.

Clearly, f is static. So the first requirement has been fulfilled. Notice, however, that for f to be generally applicable we still need to give a simple definition of $s(i)$, $i \geq n$.

According to the second requirement a node and its successors should be mapped onto different vertices. Due to the definition of f we already have $f(xa) \neq f(xb)$ and $f(x) \neq f(xa)$, for each node x. In order to obtain that $f(x) \neq f(xb)$, for each node x, we have to require that $s(i) \neq s(i-1)$, for all i, $i > 0$. We therefore confine ourselves to sequences $s(i : i \geq 0)$ satisfying

$$\forall(i : 0 \leq i < n : s(i) = i) \wedge \forall(i : n \leq i : s(i-1) \neq s(i)).$$

Consequently, the distance between the vertices on which node x and its successors xa and xb are mapped is 1 for x and xa, and 2 for x and xb. Hence, f has indeed cost 2.

The analysis concerning the third requirement is harder. As might be expected, whether two successors of two nodes of distinct height, which are mapped onto the same vertex, are also mapped onto an equal vertex, depends on the definition of $s(i), i \geq n$, and the completeness of the tree. Let x and y be two nodes with $ht(x) < ht(y)$, such that $f(x) = f(y)$. Due to the homogeneity of f for $BT(n)$, we thus have $ht(y) \geq n$. Considering the vertices on which the successors, if they exist, of x and y are mapped, we obtain $f(xa) \neq f(yb) \wedge f(xb) \neq f(ya) \wedge (f(xb) = f(yb) \Rightarrow f(xa) = f(ya))$. So, we first determine when $f(xa)$ and $f(ya)$ are the same vertex. According to the definition we have $f(x) = f(y) \Rightarrow (f(xa) = f(ya) \equiv s(ht(xa)) = s(ht(ya)))$. Hence it seems attractive to guarantee that two equal values in s are as distant as possible. Since we have $\forall(i : i \geq 0 : 0 \leq s(i) < n)$, the distance between two equal s-values is at most n. The sequence s, in which for each value j, $0 \leq j < n$, this maximal distance is obtained, is given by $\forall(i : i \geq 0 : s(i+n) = s(i))$. But, then, we also have $\forall(i : i \geq 1 : s(i-1+n) = s(i-1))$. Hence for this sequence s we get

$$f(x) = f(y) \Rightarrow f(xa) = f(ya) \wedge f(xb) = f(yb).$$

Consequently, the subtrees with root x and with root y are mapped onto the same set of vertices. For incomplete binary trees this might lead to an inhomogeneous distribution of nodes over vertices. We therefore propose a less regular sequence for s.

Since the homogeneity and the height-homogeneity of f guarantee a uniform distribution of nodes over vertices when f is applied on a complete binary tree, we next concentrate on the case where f is applied to an incomplete binary tree. In particular we consider which restrictions are to be imposed upon a sequence s in order to achieve a homogeneous distribution of nodes over vertices when f is applied to a left-skewed tree. We hope to obtain thereby a sequence s that also leads to a reasonable distribution of nodes when other incomplete binary trees are to be mapped.

So consider a left-skewed tree. On account of the definition of f we have that, for each node x, $f(x)$ and $f(xa)$ share a "left" edge of the cube. Hence, as in the previous section, in order to obtain a homogeneous mapping f for a left-skewed tree of any size, the left edges have to form a Hamiltonian cycle. By using the definition of s, we have for $0 \le i < n$

$$f(a^i) = u_i \text{ with } \forall(j : 0 \le j \le i : u_i(j) = 1) \land \forall(j : i < j < n : u_i(j) = 0).$$

Let the Hamiltonian cycle to be constructed be denoted by the sequence $Ham_n(i : 0 \le i < 2^n)$ of vertices of $BC(n)$. Then we have

$$Ham_n(i) = u_i, \text{ for } 0 \le i < n.$$

We show the existence of Ham_n by induction on n. For that purpose we introduce four operations on sequences.

- Let for $n \ge 1$ $BC(n-1) \to BC(n)$ be the homogeneous mapping of cost 1 that extends the bit pattern of a vertex of $BC(n-1)$ with a 0, i.e., $id_{n-1}(u) = v$ with $\forall(i : 0 \le i < n-1 : u(i) = v(i)) \land v(n-1) = 0$. Then we define for a sequence $c(j : 0 \le j < m)$ of vertices of $BC(n-1)$ the operation sid_{n-1} by $sid_{n-1}(c) = d$ where the sequence $d(j : 0 \le j < m)$ of vertices of $BC(n)$ satisfies $\forall(j : 0 \le j < m : d(j) = id_{n-1}(c(j)))$.

- Define for $n \ge 1$ the mapping $plus_{n-1} : BC(n-1) \to BC(n)$ by $plus_{n-1}(u) = v$, where $v \in BC(n).V$ satisfies $\forall(i : o \le i < n-1 : u(i) = v(i)) \land v(n-1) = 1$. The operation $splus_{n-1}$ is defined similarly to sid_{n-1}.

- For a sequence $c(j : 0 \le j < m)$ and n, $n \ge 0$, we denote the operation by which the elements of c are rotated n positions to the left as $rot_n(c)$, i.e., $rot_n(c) = d$, where the sequence $d(j : 0 \le j < m)$ satisfies $\forall(j : 0 \le j < m : d(j) = c((j+n) \bmod m))$.

- The operation on a sequence $c(j : 0 \leq j < m)$ by which the elements of c are obtained in reverse order is denoted by $rev(c)$, i.e., $rev(c) = d$, where the sequence $d(j : 0 \leq j < m)$ satisfies $\forall(j : 0 \leq j < m : d(j) = c(m - 1 - j))$.

Equipped with these operations the inductive proof of the existence of Ham_n reads:

$n = 1$ Define Ham_1 by $< 1, 0 >$; then $Ham_1 = u_0$

$n > 1$ Let Ham_{n-1} satisfy to $Ham_{n-1} = u_i$, for $0 \leq i < n - 1$. Then we construct Ham_n as follows:

$$Ham_n =< \quad id_{n-1}(c),$$
$$plus_{n-1}(rev(rot_{n-1}(Ham_{n-1}))),$$
$$id_{n-1}(c') >$$

where sequences $c(i : 0 \leq i < n - 1)$ and $c'(i : 0 \leq i < 2^{n-1} - (n - 1))$ of vertices of $BC(n-1)$ satisfy $< c, c' >= Ham_{n-1}$. In order to prove that Ham_n is a Hamiltonian cycle in $BC(n)$ we first notice that $rev(rot(Ham_{n-1}))$ is still a Hamiltonian cycle in $BC(n-1)$, and that id_{n-1} and $plus_{n-1}$ are embeddings of cost 1. Hence, it suffices to show that the "boundary" vertices are adjacent, i.e., to show that

$$\{id_{n-1}(c(n-2)), plus_{n-1}(d(0))\} \in BC(n).E \quad \text{and}$$
$$\{plus_{n-1}(d(2^{n-1}-1)), id_{n-1}(c'(0))\} \in BC(n).E,$$

where $d = rev(rot_{n-1}(Ham_{n-1}))$. But, since the length of c is $n - 1$ and $Ham_{n-1} =< c, c' >$, we have $rot(Ham_{n-1}) =< c', c >$, and, hence $d =< rev(c), rev(c') >$. Consequently, we have $d(0) = c(n-2) \wedge d(2^{n-1} - 1) = c'(0)$.

By using the definition of id_{n-1} and of $plus_{n-1}$ we thus obtain that Ham_n is a Hamiltonian cycle in $BC(n)$, and that Ham_n satisfies $Ham_n(i) = u_i$, for $0 \leq i < n$.

From the Hamiltonian cycle Ham_n we construct our final mapping f. Consider two successive vertices, say u and v, in this cycle. Since u and v are adjacent, they differ in exactly one bit position. This position is used to define the sequence s.

Let $diff: BC(n).E \rightarrow \{i : 0 \leq i < n\}$ be the function given by

$$diff(\{u, v\}) = i \equiv u(i) \neq v(i).$$

Then we define the sequence $s(i : i \geq 0)$ by

$$s(i) = diff(\{Ham_n((i-1) \bmod 2^n), Ham_n(i \bmod 2^n)\})$$

and f is (as before) given by

$f(\varepsilon) = 0 \cdots 01,$
$f(xa) = c_{s(i)}(f(x)),$ where $i = ht(xa)$, and
$f(xb) = (c_{s(i)} \circ c_{s(i-1)})(f(x)),$ where $i = ht(xb)$.

Recapitulating, f is homogeneous and height-homogeneous for complete, binary trees, f is homogeneous for left-skewed trees, f has cost 2, and f maps a node and its successors, if they exist, onto distinct vertices. Moreover, due to irregularity introduced by the Hamiltonian cycle, when two nodes of different heights are mapped onto the same vertex, then their successors are usually not mapped onto the same vertices. From this last property we infer that when the mapping f is applied on an incomplete binary tree, then in general a reasonable distribution of nodes over vertices is obtained.

Remark 5.18

As we have seen, the mapping f restricted to the nodes of height less than n results in a homogeneous mapping from $BT(n)$ to $BC(n)$ of cost 2, corresponding to the sequence $s'(i : 0 \leq i < n)$ defined by $s'(i) = i$, for $0 \leq i < n$. In effect we might have chosen any permutation of the set $\{i : 0 \leq i < n : i\}$ to obtain such a mapping. For instance, if we choose the "bit reversal" permutation t of s', i.e., $t(i) = s(n-1-i)$, for $0 \leq i < n$, then we obtain the mapping corresponding to the numbering of the vertices of the Sneptree $T(n)$. Since the construction of the Hamiltonian cycle Ham_n depends on s', choosing another permutation also leads to another Hamiltonian cycle. For reasons of symmetry we do not expect that the choice of the permutation affects the distribution of nodes over vertices considerably. We have, therefore, chosen the identity function as permutation.
(End of remark)

This concludes our discussion of the mapping of binary tree computation graphs. It has often been stated that the property of being Hamiltonian is an important notion in graph theory. In both sections of this chapter the Hamiltonicity has been an important factor. It comes as a surprise that, when mappings of computation graphs on implementation graphs are considered, the Hamiltonicity of the implementation graph can be that useful.

Chapter 6

Mappings on torus-connected graphs

In Chapter 3 we introduced torus-connected graphs as suitable candidates for VLSI processor networks, when latency and throughput are considered. Another criterion for processor networks concerns how readily one can construct homogeneous mappings of computation graphs on them. In this chapter we shall show that torus-connected graphs also have nice properties when homogeneous mappings are considered. In effect, a method is discussed by which, from any homogeneous mapping of an arbitrary computation graph on a torus, a homogeneous mapping of that computation graph on a torus-connected graph can be obtained.

6.1 A hierarchical mapping method

Applying the braid operation results, in general, in a graph with many vertices. Consequently, the construction of a homogeneous mapping on a braid graph is a complex task. To reduce this complexity some method is needed by which parts of a braid graph can be treated separately. In this section we describe such a method for torus-connected graphs, although the same method can be used for other braid graphs as well.

For the sake of completeness we first repeat some notions from Chapter 2. Let m be an integer, $m \geq 3$, G a graph, and α a function from $G.V$ to $\{0,1\}$. Then a torus-connected graph is a graph $b(G, R(m), \alpha)$ such that

$$b(G, R(m), \alpha).V = G.V \times (R(m).V)^{\{0,1\}},$$

and for $g, h \in G.V$ and $u, v \in (R(m).V)^{\{0,1\}}$

$$\{(g, u), (h, v)\} \in b(G, R(m), \alpha).E$$

$\equiv$

$$\{g, h\} \in G.E \wedge u = v$$

$\vee$

$$g = h \wedge \alpha(g) = 0 \wedge \{u(0), v(0)\} \in R(m).E \wedge u(1) = v(1)$$

$\vee$

$$g = h \wedge \alpha(g) = 1 \wedge u(0) = v(0) \wedge \{u(1), v(1)\} \in R(m).E.$$

In order to obtain a connected torus-connected graph, we require that α be surjective (see corollary 3.16). We further assume that G is α-vertex-transitive, so that all vertices of a torus-connected graph can be treated similarly (see theorem 3.26).

Next we consider a homogeneous mapping from a computation graph, say C, to $b(G, R(m), \alpha)$. We want to find a partitioning of $b(G, R(m), \alpha)$ into reasonably large subgraphs, such that all subgraphs can be treated in a similar way. Due to the definition of $b(G, R(m), \alpha)$ we have that the function pr from $b(G, R(m), \alpha)$ to the torus $R(m) \times R(m)$ given by

$$pr((g, u)) = u$$

is a homogeneous mapping of cost 1. This mapping might be interpreted as replacing each of the m^2 copies of graph G within $b(G, R(m), \alpha)$ by a single vertex. We therefore choose for the subgraphs mentioned above these copies of graph G, and, consequently, we obtain that the subgraphs have a torus-like interconnection pattern. Having determined the subgraphs and their interconnection pattern we next describe our method by which homogeneous mappings from C to $b(G, R(m), \alpha)$ can be obtained. It is based on first mapping C homogeneously onto the torus $R(m) \times R(m)$ and then distributing the vertices of C mapped onto a vertex of the torus homogeneously over the subgraph associated with that vertex.

Let f be a homogeneous mapping from C to $R(m) \times R(m)$. According to the definition of a homogeneous mapping and corollary 4.1 we have for each u, $u \in (R(m) \times R(m).V)$,

$$p(f) = |C.V| \text{ div } m^2 \leq N(u) \leq (|C.V| + m^2 - 1) \text{ div } m^2 = q(f)$$

$\Rightarrow \quad$ { calculus, $(x + k \cdot y) \text{ div } y = (x \text{ div } y) + k$ }

$(|C.V| \text{ div } m^2) \text{ div } |G.V| \leq N(u) \text{ div } |G.V| \wedge$

$N(u) + |G.V| - 1 \leq (|C.V| + m^2 - 1 + m^2(|G.V| - 1)) \text{ div } m^2$

$\Rightarrow \quad$ { calculus }

$|C.V| \text{ div } (m^2 \cdot |G.V|) \leq N(u) \text{ div } |G.V| \leq (N(u) + |G.V| - 1) \text{ div } |G.V|$

$\leq (|C.V| + m^2 \cdot |G.V| - 1) \text{ div } (m^2 \cdot |G.V|).$ $\qquad\qquad (*)$

Hence, let $\overline{f}$ be the mapping from C to $b(G, R(m), \alpha)$ defined by first mapping C

onto $R(m) \times R(m)$ by f and then for each u, $u \in (R(m) \times R(m)).V$, distributing the $N(u)$ vertices of C mapped onto u, homogeneously over the $|G.V|$ vertices of the form (g, u), $g \in G.V$. Then we have

$$
\begin{aligned}
& p(\overline{f}) \\
= \quad & \{ \text{ def. of } p \} \\
& \mathbf{MIN}(g, u : (g, u) \in b(G, R(m), \alpha).V : N((g, u))) \\
= \quad & \{ \text{ def. of } \overline{f} \} \\
& \mathbf{MIN}(u : u \in (R(m) \times R(m)).V : N(u) \ \mathbf{div} \ |G.V|) \\
\geq \quad & \{ (*) \} \\
& |C.V| \ \mathbf{div} \ (m^2 \cdot |G.V|)
\end{aligned}
$$

and, similarly,

$$
q(\overline{f}) \leq (|C.V| + m^2 \cdot |G.V| - 1) \ \mathbf{div} \ (m^2 \cdot |G.V|),
$$

so $\overline{f}$ is a homogeneous mapping.

Next we analyse the cost of the mapping $\overline{f}$. First, we observe that by construction $f = pr \circ \overline{f}$, so, since pr has cost 1, we have that $c(f) \leq c(\overline{f})$. Second we observe that, since we have made no assumption about the distribution of vertices within a subgraph, only an upper bound for $c(\overline{f})$ can be given. The upper bound $1 + k_G + c(f)$, corresponding to the worst possible distribution, can be derived as follows. Let $\{x, y\}$ be an edge of C, such that $c(\overline{f}) = k(\overline{f}(x), \overline{f}(y))$, where $k(\overline{f}(x), \overline{f}(y))$ denotes the distance between $\overline{f}(x)$ and $\overline{f}(y)$ in $b(G, R(m), \alpha)$. Denoting $\overline{f}(x)$ and $\overline{f}(y)$ by (g, u) and (h, v), respectively, we obtain

$$
\begin{aligned}
& c(\overline{f}) \\
= \quad & \{ \text{ theorem 3.14 } \} \\
& t_0(g, h, D(u, v)) + t_1(u, v) \\
\leq \quad & \{ \text{ property 3.10, } u = f(x) \wedge v = f(y) \} \\
& t_0(g, h, \{0, 1\}) + c(f) \\
\leq \quad & \{ \text{ def. of } t_0 \} \\
& 1 + k_G + c(f),
\end{aligned}
$$

where we have used the fact that, due to the α-vertex-transitivity of G, each vertex g of G has a neighbour g' in G with $\alpha(g) \neq \alpha(g')$ (see section 3.5), and where k_G denotes the diameter of G. Since this upper bound corresponds to the worst case situation, it is, in general, not attained. In the example below it is shown that by making adequate use of properties of both C and f a mapping $\overline{f}$ can be obtained with a cost close to $c(f)$.

Although by applying the method low cost homogeneous mappings can be achieved, there is another reason why we have introduced the method. When processor networks are considered in which off-chip links and on-chip links have to be distinguished, then in the cost of a mapping onto such a processor network a similar distinction has to be made. As mentioned in section 3.5 a torus-connected graph $b(G, R(m), \alpha)$ may be viewed as a processor network with the on-chip links described by the graph G and the off-chip links by the torus $R(m) \times R(m)$. So applying the above method results in a mapping in which the two costs are distinguished.

We end this section with an example.

Example 6.1
In this example we show that by applying the method a minimum cost homogeneous mapping from the square grid $P(6) \times P(6)$ (see example 3.44) to the torus-connected graph $b(R(4), R(3), i \bmod 2)$ (see example 3.45) can be constructed.

Suppose s is a homogeneous mapping from $P(6) \times P(6)$ to $b(R(4), R(3), i \bmod 2)$ of cost 1. Since both $P(6) \times P(6)$ and $b(R(4), R(3), i \bmod 2)$ have 36 vertices, s is a one-to-one mapping. Hence s maps each two different cycles of four vertices onto different 4-cycles. But $P(6) \times P(6)$ contains 25 different 4-cycles, whereas $b(R(4), R(3), i \bmod 2)$ has only nine different 4-cycles. Consequently, such a mapping s cannot exist. So a homogeneous mapping from $P(6) \times P(6)$ to $b(R(4), R(3), i \bmod 2)$ has cost at least 2.

Next we present a mapping $\overline{f}$ of cost 2. According to the method we first have to construct a homogeneous mapping f from $P(6) \times P(6)$ to the torus $R(3) \times R(3)$. Let f be defined by

$$f((i, j)) = (i \bmod 3, j \bmod 3), \text{ for } 0 \leq i, j < 6.$$

Then f is a homogeneous mapping from $P(6) \times P(6)$ to the torus $R(3) \times R(3)$ of cost 1. Consequently, four vertices of $P(6) \times P(6)$ are mapped by f onto a vertex u of $R(3) \times R(3)$. Following the method we next have to distribute the four vertices mapped onto u over the four vertices of the subgraph $(R(4), u)$ of $b(R(4), R(3), i \bmod 2)$. In order to obtain a cost 2 mapping we observe that the distance in $b(R(4), R(3), i \bmod 2)$ between (g, u) and (h, v) is 2, for $g \bmod 2 \neq h \bmod 2$ and u and v adjacent in $R(3) \times R(3)$. Furthermore, if $\{(i, j), (k, l)\}$ is an edge in $P(6) \times P(6)$, then we have that $(i + j) \bmod 2 \neq (k + l) \bmod 2$. So, to construct a homogeneous mapping $\overline{f}$ of cost 2, it suffices to assign the vertex (i, j) mapped by f onto u to a vertex (g, u) of $(R(4), u)$ satisfying $g \bmod 2 = (i + j) \bmod 2$. Denote the vertex u of

$R(3) \times R(3)$ by (x, y). Then the vertices of $P(6) \times P(6)$ mapped onto (x, y) are $(x, y), (x + 3, y + 3), (x, y + 3)$, and $(x + 3, y)$, and a mapping $\overline{f}$, satisfying the above requirement is given by

$$\overline{f}(x, y) = ((x + y) \bmod 2, (x, y)),$$
$$\overline{f}(x + 3, y + 3) = (2 + (x + y) \bmod 2, (x, y)),$$
$$\overline{f}(x, y + 3) = (1 - (x + y) \bmod 2, (x, y)), \text{ and}$$
$$\overline{f}(x + 3, y) = (3 - (x + y) \bmod 2, (x, y)).$$

(End of example)

In the following section we show that the method does not always lead to minimum cost mappings.

6.2 Mappings of linear arrays onto $b(R(2n), R(2m), i \bmod 2)$

In the previous chapter we saw that the property of having a Hamiltonian cycle might be important for processor networks. In this section we show that a linear array of any size can be homogeneously mapped on $b(R(n), R(m), i \bmod 2)$, for n and m even, with cost 1 by proving that these graphs possess a Hamiltonian cycle. We restrict our attention to graphs $b(R(n), R(m), i \bmod 2)$ with n and m even, because

- on account of corollary 3.27 $b(R(n), R(m), i \bmod 2)$ is vertex-transitive for even n only,

- due to the smaller bisection width (see section 3.5) the graphs $b(G, R(2k), \alpha)$ are more attractive as processor networks than the graphs $b(G, R(2k + 1), \alpha)$, and

- the simplest graphs of the form $b(G, R(m), \alpha)$ such that G has a Hamiltonian cycle with a different α-value for the initial and terminal vertices of the cycle are the graphs $b(R(n), R(m), i \bmod 2)$.

Before proving the Hamiltonicity of $b(R(2n), R(2m), i \bmod 2)$ we show by an example that the method proposed in the previous section does not always result in minimum cost homogeneous mappings.

Example 6.2

Let C be the linear array with three vertices, i.e., $C = P(3)$, and G be the graph $b(R(2), R(2), i \textbf{ mod } 2)$. Notice that, since G is isomorphic to the ring graph $R(8)$ a minimum cost homogeneous mapping from C to G has cost 1. In this example we show that applying the method of the previous section results in a homogeneous mapping of cost 2.

Let f be a homogeneous mapping from C to $R(2) \times R(2)$ of cost 1. Due to the vertex-transitivity of $R(2) \times R(2)$ we may assume that

$$f(0) = (0,0), \quad f(1) = (0,1), \quad \text{and} \quad f(2) = (1,1).$$

Consequently, mapping $\overline{f}$ from C to $b(R(2), R(2), i \textbf{ mod } 2)$ is given by

$$\overline{f}(0) = (g_0, (0,0)), \quad \overline{f}(1) = (g_1, (0,1)), \quad \text{and} \quad \overline{f}(2) = (g_2, (1,1)).$$

From

$\quad \overline{f}$ has cost 1
$\Rightarrow \quad \{ \text{ def. of } b(R(2), R(2), i \textbf{ mod } 2) \}$
$\quad\quad g_0 = g_1 = 1 \land g_1 = g_2 = 0$
$=$

$\quad false$

we deduce that $\overline{f}$ has cost at least 2. By taking $g_0 = g_1 = 1$ and $g_2 = 0$, a mapping $\overline{f}$ of cost 2 is obtained, so the minimum cost of $\overline{f}$ is 2. Notice that a similar proof can be given to show that by applying the method a homogeneous mapping $\overline{f}$ from $P(m+1)$ to $b(R(n), R(m), i \textbf{ mod } 2)$ is obtained, which has cost at least 2. (End of example)

Next we prove that $b(R(2n), R(2m), i \textbf{ mod } 2)$ has a Hamiltonian cycle. Following the method of the previous section we first investigate whether the torus $R(2m) \times R(2m)$ has a suitable Hamiltonian cycle. For that purpose we observe that $R(2n)$ has Hamiltonian cycles $x(i : 0 \leq i \leq 2n)$ such that $x(0) \textbf{ mod } 2 \neq x(2n-1) \textbf{ mod } 2$. When these cycles are used as part of the Hamiltonian cycle that is to be constructed, then we have as path in $b(R(2n), R(2m), i \textbf{ mod } 2)$

$$(x(0), u) \cdots (x(2n-1), u), (x(2n-1), u'), \cdots (x(0), u'), (x(0), u'')$$

where u, u', and $u'' \in R(2m)^{\{0,1\}}$ satisfy

$$u(j) = u'(j), \qquad\qquad \text{for } j \neq x(2n-1) \bmod 2,$$
$$\{u(j), u'(j)\} \in R(2m).E, \quad \text{for } j = x(2n-1) \bmod 2,$$
$$u'(j) = u''(j), \qquad\qquad \text{for } j \neq x(0) \bmod 2, \text{ and}$$
$$\{u'(j), u''(j)\} \in R(2m).E, \quad \text{for } j = x(0) \bmod 2,$$

with $0 \leq j < 2$. Let the edges of $R(2m) \times R(2m)$ of the form $\{(k,l), ((k+1) \bmod 2m, l)\}$ be called the horizontal edges and let the other edges of $R(2m) \times R(2m)$ be called the vertical edges. Using the projection mapping pr from $b(R(2n), R(2m), i \bmod 2)$ to $R(2m) \times R(2m)$ that was defined in the previous section, the above path is projected onto u, u', u''. Hence, when the Hamiltonian cycles of $R(2n)$ are used, then $R(2m) \times R(2m)$ has to possess a Hamiltonian cycle of alternating horizontal and vertical edges. In figure 6.3 it is shown that $R(4) \times R(4)$ has indeed such a cycle.

(0,0)   (1,0)   (2,0)   (3,0)

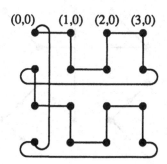

Figure 6.3: An alternating horizontal and vertical Hamiltonian cycle

For the torus $R(2m) \times R(2m)$ the Hamiltonian cycle $y(i : 0 \leq i \leq 4m^2)$ of alternating horizontal and vertical edges is defined by

$$y(4mk + 4l) = (2l, 2k), \qquad\qquad y(4mk + 4l + 1) = (2l+1, 2k),$$
$$y(4mk + 4l + 2) = (2l+1, 2k+1), \quad y(4mk + 4l + 3) = (2l+2, 2k+1),$$

where $0 \leq k \leq m$ and $0 \leq l < m$. Notice that $\{y(2i), y(2i+1)\}$ is a horizontal edge and $\{y(2i+1), y(2i+2)\}$ is a vertical edge for $0 \leq i < 2m^2$.

The final step in the construction of the Hamiltonian cycle $z(i : 0 \leq i \leq 2n \cdot 4m^2)$ of $b(R(2n), R(2m), i \bmod 2)$ is to replace each vertex u of $R(2m) \times R(2m)$ by the path $v(i : 0 \leq i < 2n)$ in $b(R(2n), R(2m), i \bmod 2)$ for $u = y(2k+1)$, $0 \leq k < 2m^2$, and by the path $v'(i : 0 \leq i < 2n)$ for $u = y(2k)$, $0 \leq k < 2m^2$, where v and v' are defined by

$$v(i) = (i, u) \text{ and } v'(i) = (2n - (i+1), u).$$

Hence v corresponds to traversing the vertices of $R(2n)$ in increasing order, while v' traverses the vertices in decreasing order. Formally, z is defined by

$$z(0) = (0, (0, 0)),$$
$$z(k \cdot 4n + i + 1) = (i, y(2k + 1)), \qquad \text{for } 0 \leq i < 2n, \text{ and}$$
$$z(k \cdot 4n + i + 1) = (4n - (i + 1), y(2k + 2)), \quad \text{for } 2n \leq i < 4n,$$

where $0 \leq k < 2m^2$. The Hamiltonian cycle z of $b(R(4), R(2), i \bmod 2)$ has been depicted in figure 6.4, where directions have been assigned to edges to show the traversal of the copies of $R(4)$.

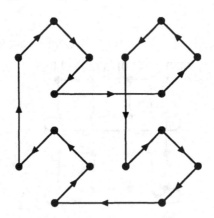

Figure 6.4: A Hamiltonian cycle of $b(R(4), R(2), i \bmod 2)$

This concludes our discussion of mappings on torus-connected graphs. The methods presented in this chapter show that braid graphs are also attractive candidates for processor networks when homogeneous mappings from computation graphs are considered.

Chapter 7

Deadlock-Free Message Routing in Processor Networks

The implementation of a computation graph on a processor network requires a routing algorithm that is deadlock-free. Many routing algorithms proposed for processor networks have the potential of deadlock due to the cyclic topology of the network. There are even commercially available routing algorithms which suffer from deadlock. In this chapter we first formalize the concept of message routing. Next, we show a method by which a deadlock-free routing algorithm can be constructed out of a given routing algorithm. Finally the method is illustrated by constructing deadlock-free routing algorithms for cartesian product processor networks. More specifically we show that by applying our method a well-known deadlock-free routing algorithm for hypercubes is obtained. In a slightly different form the contents of this chapter also appeared in [Hilb90].

7.1 Message routing

In this section some fundamental concepts of message routing in a processor network are formulated. Our approach is inspired by the work of Dally and Seitz ([Dall89]), but they considered deterministic routing algorithms only. We are concerned with general routing algorithms, and some refinements and improvements for the deterministic case are given.

As in [Dall89, Dall86a] we define routing in terms of the channels a message travels along in order to arrive at its destination. Defining routing in terms of channels has some advantages. First, multiple channels between two nodes can be distinguished. Second, it allows us to develop a method for the construction of deadlock-free routing algorithms by using the concept of virtual channels.

Our method differs from other approaches in three aspects.

(i) Our method is applicable to both wormhole routing and store-and-forward routing (see section 2.3). Günther's method ([Gunt81]) for store-and-forward routing restricts the assignment of buffers to messages. Since messages may not become interleaved when wormhole routing is used, this method is not directly applicable to wormhole routing. In our method only the paths a message may follow are restricted, so it is superimposable on either routing technique.

(ii) In other approaches ([Gunt81, Bodl86, Cido87]) the occurrence of deadlock in a processor network is defined in terms of the presence of a message in a queue at a certain moment in time. We, however, abstain from any time concept and we only assume

   (a) progress assumption: among the messages waiting for a free channel one is selected and transmitted over the channel.

   (b) release assumption: when a message has been transferred from one channel to another, queue space in the former channel is eventually released.

   (c) causality assumption: the receipt of a message is preceded by its transmission.

(iii) We show that in our method "starvation in wealth" ([Gunt81]) cannot occur, despite the fact that FIFO-scheduling may be used. This also justifies the use of the term queue instead of the commonly used term buffer.

We start with some definitions concerning relations.

Let B be a set. A relation R on B is a subset of $B \times B$.
For a relation R on B we define for $i \geq 1$
$R^0 = \{x : x \in B : (x, x)\}$,
$R^i = \{x, y : x, y \in B \wedge \exists(z : z \in B : (x, z) \in R \wedge (z, y) \in R^{i-1}) : (x, y)\}$,
$R^+ = \bigcup(i : i \geq 1 : R^i)$, and
$R^* = \bigcup(i : i \geq 0 : R^i)$,
where $\bigcup$ denotes union.
A relation R is called irreflexive iff $\forall(x : x \in B : (x, x) \notin R)$, and R is called transitive iff $\forall(x, y, z : x, y, z \in B : (x, y) \in R \wedge (y, z) \in R \Rightarrow (x, z) \in R)$.

In order to formalize the concept of message routing we have to adapt our definition of a processor network.

A *directed graph* G is a 4-tuple $< G.V, G.E, s, t >$, where $G.V$ is a non-empty set, $G.E$ is a set, and s and t are functions from $G.E$ to $G.V$. The elements of $G.V$ and $G.E$ are called nodes and edges, respectively. For each edge u, $s.u$ denotes the source node of u and $t.u$ the target node. An edge v with $s.v = t.v$ is called a self-loop.

A *processor network* is an edge-weighted, directed graph with at each node n exactly two self-loops, which are denoted by $from.n$ and $to.n$, such that

$\quad \forall(n :: cap.(from.n) = \infty \wedge cap.(to.n) = \infty)$,
$\quad \forall(u :: cap.u > 0)$, and
$\quad$ for all nodes k, n with $k \in mess.n$, a path from $from.k$ to $to.n$ exists,

where for each node n, $mess.n$ denotes the set of nodes that may generate messages destined for n, and for each edge u, the weight of edge u is denoted by $cap.u$.

Note
Unless stated otherwise, the letters $k, l,$ and n denote nodes and letters $u, v,$ and w denote edges. If no ambiguity can arise we omit the domain of these variables. (End of note)

As motivated in the introduction we describe routing in terms of the edges. We therefore assume that only edges can contain messages. For each edge u, $cap.u$ has been introduced to denote the queue space i.e. the number of messages an edge can contain, where a message is considered to be the smallest unit of information an edge can contain. Further, we require that an edge can contain at least one message.

The interaction between nodes and edges is described as follows. For all nodes k and n,

- A message produced by node k is added to the edge $from.k$, and only messages produced by node k are on $from.k$.

- Only messages destined for node n are on $to.n$ and the deletion of a message from edge $to.n$ is considered to be the consumption of a message by node n .

Instead of the assumption that a message arriving at its destination is eventually consumed, we have required that for each node n the edge $to.n$ can contain infinitely many messages. For reasons of symmetry and to express the rôle of flow control as well, we have also required that, for all nodes k, $cap.(from.k)$ be infinite.

It is usually assumed that each pair of nodes may send messages to each other, resulting in the requirement that the graph be strongly connected. We, however, do not assume that messages can be sent between each pair of nodes. Instead we have defined the notion *mess.n* for each node n, and require that for all nodes k and n with $k \in mess.n$ a path from $from.k$ to $to.n$ exist.

The next concept we formalize concerns the path a message follows in order to arrive at its destination. In our model a routing algorithm prescribes for a message with destination n, and contained in edge u, which edges can be the next on a path to $to.n$. Since many paths from u to $to.n$ may exist, there may be many such edges.

For all nodes k and n with $k \in mess.n$ the routing algorithm has to provide a path from $from.k$ to $to.n$. Further, a message is not allowed to visit an edge twice on a path from its source to its destination. These considerations are captured in the following definition of a routing algorithm for a processor network.

A *routing algorithm* R for P defines for every node n of P a relation $R.n$ on $P.E$ such that

$$(u,v) \in R.n \Rightarrow t.u = s.v,$$
$$k \in mess.n \Rightarrow (from.k, to.n) \in R.n^*,$$
$$(u,v) \in R.n \Rightarrow \exists(k : k \in mess.n : (from.k, u) \in R.n^* \land (v, to.n) \in R.n^*),$$
$$(u,u) \notin R.n^+,$$
$$(to.k, v) \notin R.n, \text{ and}$$
$$(u, from.k) \notin R.n$$

hold, for all $k \in P.V$ and $u, v \in P.E$.

We also define for a routing algorithm R

$$(u,v) \in R \equiv \exists(n :: (u,v) \in R.n).$$

Remark 7.1
The third requirement in the above definition serves to eliminate the superfluous elements in $R.n$. If R is such that all but the third requirement are satisfied then R can be made into a routing algorithm by removing those elements (u, v) from $R.n$ for which the third predicate does not hold.
(End of remark)

We end this section with two important aspects of a routing algorithm, viz. cyclicity and determinism, that are used extensively in following sections.

A routing algorithm R is called *acyclic* iff $\forall(u :: (u, u) \notin R^+)$ and R is called *deterministic* iff $\forall(n, u : u \neq to.n : N(v :: (u, v) \in R.n) = 1)$.

7.2 Deadlock-free routing algorithms

In this section we first consider the notion of deadlock. Then we present a simple, sufficient condition for a routing algorithm to be deadlock-free. Next we show a method for constructing a deadlock-free routing algorithm out of an arbitrary routing algorithm. Finally, we illustrate the method by constructing a deadlock-free routing algorithm for two simple processor networks, viz. the complete network and the ring network.

Let P be a processor network. From now on we restrict ourselves to processor networks with finitely many edges and we identify a message with its destination node. We denote the set of self-loops of P as $P.S$:

$$P.S \;=\; \{k :: from.k\} \;\cup\; \{n :: to.n\}.$$

For all nodes n and edges u, we define the predicate *admissible* by

$$admissible.n.u \equiv \exists(k: k \in mess.n : (from.k, u) \in R.n^* \wedge (u, to.n) \in R.n^*).$$

A *configuration* is a function f from $P.V \times P.E$ to $\mathbb{N}$ such that

$$\forall(n, u :: (f.n.u > 0 \Rightarrow admissible.n.u) \wedge size.u \leq cap.u),$$

where for each edge u, $size.u$ is defined as $size.u = S(n :: f.n.u)$.

A configuration is called non-empty iff $\exists(u : u \notin P.S : size.u > 0)$.

Notice that $f.n.u$ denotes the number of messages destined for n present on edge u. Next the definition of a deadlock-free routing algorithm is given.

A routing algorithm R is *deadlock-free* iff for every non-empty configuration

$$\exists(u: size.u > 0: \forall(n: admissible.n.u: \exists(v: (u, v) \in R.n: size.v < cap.v))).$$

Hence, given a deadlock-free routing algorithm and a non-empty configuration an edge u exists such that at least one message on u can be forwarded, provided a non-full edge v is selected by the routing algorithm.

A sufficient condition for a routing algorithm to be deadlock-free is presented in the following theorem.

Theorem 7.2
An acyclic routing algorithm is deadlock-free.

Proof
Let R be an acyclic routing algorithm. Consider an arbitrary non-empty configuration and let B denote the set of all edges v with $size.v = cap.v$. We have to show the existence of an edge u with $size.u > 0$ satisfying $\forall(n : admissible.n.u : \exists(v : (u,v) \in R.n : size.v < cap.v))$. If B is the empty set, then the existence is clear. Hence suppose B is non-empty. According to the definition of an acyclic routing algorithm we have $\forall(u :: (u,u) \notin R^+)$. Since B is finite, there exists an edge u in B which is maximal with respect to R^+, i.e. $\forall(v : v \in B : \neg(u,v) \in R^+)$. Edge u cannot be an element of $P.S$, because $cap.u = size.u$. Let n satisfy $admissible.n.u$; then we have $(u, to.n) \in R.n^+$. According to the definition of $R.n^+$, this implies that $\exists(v :: (u,v) \in R.n)$. Such an edge v is not an element of B, for u is maximal in B with respect to R^+. Thus $size.v < cap.v$.
(End of proof and theorem)

Notice that we have proved an even stronger theorem, viz.

  R is acyclic
$\Rightarrow$
  for every non-empty configuration
  $\exists(u : size.u > 0 : \forall(n : admissible.n.u : \forall(v : (u,v) \in R.n : size.v < cap.v)))$.

Hence, given an acyclic routing algorithm and a non-empty configuration, an edge u exists such that at least one message on u can be forwarded independent of which edge v is selected by the routing algorithm. Since the selection of which message on u is transmitted first is not relevant, starvation in wealth is impossible when FIFO-scheduling is used.

A routing algorithm is not necessarily acyclic, as may be concluded from the following example.

Example 7.3
Consider the following deadlocked processor network:

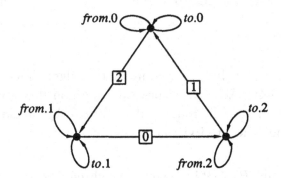

Figure 7.4: A deadlocked processor network

where $mess.0 = \{1\}$, $mess.1 = \{2\}$, $mess.2 = \{0\}$,
$R.0 = \{(from.1, (1,2)), ((1,2), (2,0)), ((2,0), to.0)\}$,
$R.1 = \{(from.2, (2,0)), ((2,0), (0,1)), ((0,1), to.1)\}$, and
$R.2 = \{(from.0, (0,1)), ((0,1), (1,2)), ((1,2), to.2)\}$, and all edges except the self-loops have capacity 1. The queue associated with an edge has been represented by a box on that edge and the figures in boxes denote a message present on an edge. R is not acyclic since, for example, $((0,1), (0,1)) \in R^+$.
(End of example)

The converse of theorem 7.2 is in general not true. There exist deadlock-free routing algorithms that are not acyclic:

Example 7.5
Add an extra edge u with source node 0 and target node 1, and capacity 1 to the processor network of example 7.3 and add $\{((2,0), u), (u, to.1)\}$ to $R.1$. One can verify that R is deadlock-free.
(End of example)

If, however, R is also deterministic, then we have:

Theorem 7.6

A deterministic routing algorithm R is deadlock-free iff R is acyclic.

Proof

See [Dall89, Dall86a] with the improved definitions of a routing algorithm and a configuration.

(End of proof and theorem)

From example 7.3 we may conclude that many routing algorithms are cyclic due to the cyclic topology of the network. Next we present a method that given a cyclic routing algorithm R constructs an acyclic routing algorithm R' by breaking the cycles. The method is based on the concept of virtual edges.

Virtual processor network P' of P is the edge-weighted directed graph P' with
$P'.V = P.V,$
$P'.E = \{u,i : u \in P.E \wedge \neg(u \in P.S) \wedge i \geq 0 : (u,i)\} \cup P.S,$
$\forall(u,i : (u,i) \in P'.E : s'.(u,i) = s.u), \forall(k :: s'.from.k = k \wedge s'.to.k = k),$
$\forall(u,i : (u,i) \in P'.E : t'.(u,i) = t.u), \forall(k :: t'.from.k = k \wedge t'.to.k = k),$
$\forall(u' : u' \in P'.E : cap'.u' > 0),$
$\forall(u' : u' \in P'.S : cap'.u' = \infty),$ and
$\forall(n :: mess'.n = mess.n)$
where for each edge u', the weight of edge u' is denoted as $cap'.u'$.

Notice that for all nodes k and n, with $k \in mess'.n$, a path from $from.k$ to $to.n$ exists, and that each node has exactly two self-loops. For virtual edge (u,i) we refer to u as the edge and to i as the level.

We use the more convenient notation $u < v$ instead of writing $(u,v) \in <$, for a relation $<$ on $P.E$. Let $<$ be an irreflexive, transitive relation on $P.E$. Then we define:

The routing algorithm R' induced by R and $<$ on P' is the routing algorithm that is constructed as follows. For all $k,n \in P'.V$, $u,v \in P.E - P.S$, and $i \geq 0$ we define the relation $R'.n$ on $P'.E$ by

$$
\begin{array}{lcl}
\text{-} \ (from.k,(v,i)) \in R'.n & \equiv & (from.k,v) \in R.n \wedge i = 0, \\
\text{-} \ ((u,i),to.n) \in R'.n & \equiv & (u,to.n) \in R.n, \\
\text{-} \ ((u,i),(v,i)) \in R'.n & \equiv & (u,v) \in R.n \wedge u < v, \\
\text{-} \ ((u,i),(v,i+1)) \in R'.n & \equiv & (u,v) \in R.n \wedge \neg(u < v), \\
\text{-} \ (from.k,to.n) \in R'.n & \equiv & (from.k,to.n) \in R.n,
\end{array}
$$

and remove from $R'.n$ those (u',v') for which $\neg\, admissible.n.u' \lor \neg\, admissible.n.v'$ holds. The relation thus obtained is again denoted by $R'.n$.

Theorem 7.7
R' is acyclic.

Proof
Suppose R' is cyclic. Let γ' be a cycle. For each u', $u' \in \gamma'$, we have that $u' \notin P'.S$ according to the fact that R' is a routing algorithm. Hence each such u' is of the form (u, i) for some $u \in P.E - P.S$ and $i \geq 0$. All elements in the cycle must have the same level, since this level never decreases. But using the transitivity of $<$, this leads to $u < u$ which is in contradiction with the irreflexitivity of $<$.
(End of proof and theorem)

Two remaining problems have to do with the relation $<$ on $P.E$ and the number of levels needed. We start with the latter problem. Let γ be an R-path from $from.k$ to $to.n$, with $k \in mess.n$, i.e. γ is a path $u_0, \ldots, u_m$ in P with $u_0 = from.k$, $u_m = to.n$, and $\forall(j : 0 < j \leq m : (u_{j-1}, u_j) \in R.n)$. Define $l(\gamma) = \mathbf{N}(j : 0 < j < m : \neg(u_{j-1} < u_j)) + 1$. Let M be the maximal $l(\gamma)$. Then M levels are needed. On the level of implementation this means that each physical edge must have a capacity of at least M.

When we apply the method to an acyclic routing algorithm R with R^+ for $<$, we get $M = 1$, and

$$P'.E \;=\; \{u : u \in P.E - P.S : (u, 0)\} \cup P.S.$$

Hence $P'.E \simeq P.E$, and $R' \simeq R$, where $\simeq$ denotes set-isomorphism.

Next we consider the relation $<$ on $P.E$. We assume that distinct static numbers are assigned to the nodes of P, such that $<$ is a total relation on $P.V$. For $(u, v) \in R$ we define $<$ on $P.E$ by

$$u < v \;\equiv\; s.u < t.u \lor s.v > t.v,$$

where $>$ is defined by $k > l \equiv l < k$. Hence $<$ may be viewed as the set

$$\{u, v : u, v \in P.E \land (s.u < t.u \lor s.v > t.v) : (u, v)\} \cap R.$$

Although $u < v \land v < w \Rightarrow s.u < t.u \lor s.w > t.w$, $<$ is not necessarily transitive, since $(u, v) \in R \land (v, w) \in R$ does not imply that $(u, w) \in R$. Therefore we consider the transitive closure of $<$, which is denoted by $<^+$.

Lemma 7.8

$\forall(u :: \neg(u <^+ u))$.

Proof

Suppose $u <^+ u$ holds. Let $u = u_0, \ldots, u_i = u$ be a $<$-cycle i.e. $\forall(j : 0 \leq j < i : u_j < u_{j+1})$ holds. Then we have (with subscripts reduced modulo i)

$\qquad \forall(j : 0 \leq j < i : u_j < u_{j+1})$

$= \qquad \{$ definition of $< \}$

$\qquad \forall(j : 0 \leq j < i : (u_j, u_{j+1}) \in R) \wedge$
$\qquad \forall(j : 0 \leq j < i : s.u_j < t.u_j \vee s.u_{j+1} > t.u_{j+1})$

$\Rightarrow \qquad \{ i \geq 2, \text{ since } \neg(u < u) \text{ holds } \}$

$\qquad \forall(j : 0 \leq j < i : t.u_j = s.u_{j+1}) \wedge \forall(j : 0 \leq j < i : u_j \notin P.S) \wedge$
$\qquad \forall(j : 0 \leq j < i : s.u_j < t.u_j \vee s.u_{j+1} > t.u_{j+1})$

$\Rightarrow$

$\qquad \forall(j : 0 \leq j < i : t.u_{j-1} < t.u_j \vee t.u_j > t.u_{j+1})$

$=$

$\qquad \forall(j : 0 \leq j < i : \min(t.u_{j-1}, t.u_{j+1}) < t.u_j)$

$\Rightarrow \qquad \{$ choose h such that $t.u_h = \mathbf{MIN}(j : 0 \leq j < i : t.u_j)\}$

$\qquad \min(t.u_{h-1}, t.u_{h+1}) < t.u_h$

$=$

$\qquad false.$

(End of proof and lemma)

Since the transitive closure preserves the subset relation, we have that $u <^+ v \equiv u < v$ for $(u, v) \in R$ holds which justifies the use of $<$ instead of $<^+$ in the examples below.

We end this section with two examples, which are used in the next section. For the sake of convenience we do not consider the capacities of the edges, and we assume that a node may generate messages destined for any node.

Example 7.9 *the complete processor network*

The complete processor network with N nodes is defined by

$P.V = \{k : 0 \leq k < N : k\}$, and
$P.E = \{k, l : k \neq l : (k, l)\} \cup \{k :: from.k\} \cup \{n :: to.n\}$.

For each node n, $R.n$ is given by

$$R.n = \{k : k \neq n : (from.k, (k, n))\} \cup \{k : k \neq n : ((k, n), to.n)\}.$$

Obviously, R is acyclic. Hence R is deadlock-free, and only one level is needed. (End of example)

As has been shown in example 7.3, the ring network is less trivial.

Example 7.10 *the ring network*
We start with the unidirectional ring P_u with at least three nodes. P_u consists of N nodes, numbered from 0 through $N - 1$, and edges $(k, k + 1)$, $from.k$, and $to.k$, for $0 \leq k < N$. Throughout this example we assume that addition and subtraction are performed modulo N.

For each node n, $0 \leq n < N$, $R.n$ is given by

$$R.n = \{k : k \neq n : (from.k, (k, k+1))\} \cup \{k : k \neq n : ((k - 1, k), (k, k+1))\}$$
$$\cup \{((n - 1, n), to.n)\}.$$

In terms of an algorithm, let u be an edge with $t.u = k$ and $u \neq to.n$:

if $k \neq n \;\; \to v := (k, k + 1)$
[] $k = n \;\; \to v := to.n$
fi .

As can easily be seen R is cyclic. We apply our method with $u < v \;\equiv\; s.u < t.u \vee s.v > t.v$. We first calculate M. The only element (u, v) in R with $\neg(u < v)$ is $((N - 1, 0), (0, 1))$, so only two levels are needed. Hence $R'.n$ can be constructed as follows. Let u' be an edge with $t'.u' = k$ and $k \neq n$.

If $k \neq 0$ we have

if $u' = from.k \qquad\qquad \to v' := ((k, k + 1), 0)$
[] $u' = ((k - 1, k), 0) \quad \to v' := ((k, k + 1), 0)$
[] $u' = ((k - 1, k), 1) \quad \to v' := ((k, k + 1), 1)$
fi ,

and, if $k = 0$ we have

$$
\begin{array}{lll}
\textbf{if} & u' = from.0 & \rightarrow v' := (\,(0,1),0\,) \\
\textbf{[]} & u' = (\,(N-1,0),0\,) & \rightarrow v' := (\,(0,1),1\,) \\
\textbf{fi} \; .
\end{array}
$$

Next we consider the bidirectional ring P_b. In the unidirectional ring only routing in "clockwise" direction is allowed. In P_b routing of messages in "anticlockwise" direction is also allowed.

P_b consists of N nodes, numbered $0 \ldots (N-1)$, and edges $from.k$, $to.k$, $(k, \; k-1\,)$, and $(k, k+1)$, for each k, $0 \leq k < N$. We describe $R.n$ in terms of an algorithm. Let u be an edge with $t.u \neq n$ and $t.u = k$.

$$
\begin{array}{lll}
\textbf{if} \; k < n & \rightarrow l := n - k \;;\; r := N + k - n \\
\textbf{[]} \; k > n & \rightarrow l := N + n - k \;;\; r := k - n \\
\textbf{fi} \\
\textbf{if} \; u = from.k \;\wedge\; l \geq r & \rightarrow v := (k, k-1) \\
\textbf{[]} \; u = from.k \;\wedge\; l \leq r & \rightarrow v := (k, k+1) \\
\textbf{[]} \; u = (k-1, k) & \rightarrow v := (k, k+1) \\
\textbf{[]} \; u = (k+1, k) & \rightarrow v := (k, k-1) \\
\textbf{fi.}
\end{array}
$$

If $t.u = n \wedge u \neq to.n$ we have $v := to.n$.

Again it is clear that R is not acyclic. In calculating M we notice that the elements (u, v) of R with $\neg(u < v)$ are $(\,(N\text{-}1,0),(0,1)\,)$, and $(\,(1,0),(0,N\text{-}1)\,)$. But they do not both occur in an R-path from a $from.k$ to some $to.n$. Hence, again, two levels are sufficient. Presumably, this was also meant in algorithm 3 in [Gunt81]. Now we can describe $R'.n$.

Let u' be an edge with $t'.u' = k$ and $k \neq n$. Let i be an integer with $0 \leq i \leq 1$, and let l and r be defined as above.

For $k \neq 0$ the algorithm is

$$\textbf{if} \quad u' = from.k \wedge l \geq r \quad \rightarrow v' := (\,(k, k-1), 0\,)$$
$$[\!] \quad u' = from.k \wedge l \leq r \quad \rightarrow v' := (\,(k, k+1), 0\,)$$
$$[\!] \quad u' = (\,(k-1, k), i\,) \quad \rightarrow v' := (\,(k, k+1), i\,)$$
$$[\!] \quad u' = (\,(k+1, k), i\,) \quad \rightarrow v' := (\,(k, k-1), i\,)$$
$$\textbf{fi,}$$

and for $k = 0$

$$\textbf{if} \quad u' = from.0 \wedge l \geq r \quad \rightarrow v' := (\,(0, N-1), 0\,)$$
$$[\!] \quad u' = from.0 \wedge l \leq r \quad \rightarrow v' := (\,(0, 1), 0\,)$$
$$[\!] \quad u' = (\,(N-1, 0), 0\,) \quad \rightarrow v' := (\,(0, 1), 1\,)$$
$$[\!] \quad u' = (\,(1, 0), 0\,) \quad \rightarrow v' := (\,(0, N-1), 1\,)$$
$$\textbf{fi.}$$

(End of example)

7.3 Routing in cartesian product processor networks

Various networks proposed as parallel computer architecture have the property of being the cartesian product of smaller processor networks. In this section we investigate the method in connection with the cartesian product operator. For a processor network that is the cartesian product of processor networks $P0$ and $P1$ with $M0$ and $M1$ levels, respectively, we construct a deadlock-free routing algorithm requiring $M0$ **max** $M1$ levels. This construction is believed to be new. We start with the definition of the cartesian product for processor networks.

Let $P0$ and $P1$ be processor networks. The *cartesian product processor network* P of $P0$ and $P1$ is the processor network with

- $P.V = P0.V \times P1.V$,
- $P.E = (P0.E - P0.S) \times P1.V \ \cup \ P0.V \times (P1.E - P1.S)$
  $\cup \{k, l : k \in P0.V \wedge l \in P1.V : from.(k, l)\}$
  $\cup \{k, l : k \in P0.V \wedge l \in P1.V : to.(k, l)\}$,
- $s.(u, l) = (s0.u, l)$, $t.(u, l) = (t0.u, l)$,
- $s.(k, v) = (k, s1.v)$, $t.(k, v) = (k, t1.v)$,
- $s.from.(k, l) = (k, l)$, $t.to.(k, l) = (k, l)$, and
- $mess.(k, l) = mess.k \times mess.l$,
for $u \in P0.E - P0.S$, $v \in P1.E - P1.S$, $k \in P0.V$, and $l \in P1.V$.

Next we develop a routing algorithm R for cartesian product processor network P. Suppose $(k, l) \in mess.(m, n)$, and let $R0$ and $R1$ be routing algorithms for $P0$ and $P1$, respectively.

Since $k \in mess.m$, an $R0$-path γ_0 in $P0$ from $from.k$ to $to.m$ exists, i.e. γ_0 is a path $u_0, \ldots, u_p$ in $P0$ with $u_0 = from.k$, $u_p = to.m$, and $\forall(j : 0 < j \leq p : (u_{j-1}, u_j) \in R0.m)$. We transform γ_0 into a path $\gamma_0' = w_0, \ldots, w_{p-1}$ in P by defining $w_0 = from.(k, l)$ and $\forall(j : 0 < j < p : w_j = (u_j, l))$. Notice that since $(u_{p-1}, to.m) \in R0.m$, the target node of u_{p-1} is m.

Since $l \in mess.n$, an $R1$-path $\gamma_1 = v_0, \ldots, v_q$ in $P1$ from $from.l$ to $to.n$ exists. We transform γ_1 into a path $\gamma_1' = w_p, \ldots, w_{p+q-1}$ in P by defining $\forall(j : 0 < j < q : w_{p+j-1} = (m, v_j))$ and $w_{p+q-1} = to.(m, n)$.

Let γ be the concatenation of γ_0' and γ_1'. Then γ is a path in P from $from.(k, l)$ to $to.(m, n)$. Routing algorithm R is defined to describe such paths.

Routing algorithm R for the cartesian product network P is defined by

$R.(m, n)$
$=$
$\quad \{k, l, u : l \in P1.V \wedge (from.k, u) \in R0.m \wedge u \notin P0.S : (from.(k, l), (u, l))\}$
$\quad \cup \{l, v : (from.l, v) \in R1.n \wedge v \notin P1.S : (from.(m, l), (m, v))\}$
$\quad \cup \{u : (u, to.m) \in R0.m \wedge u \notin P0.S : ((u, n), to.(m, n))\}$
$\quad \cup \{v : (v, to.n) \in R1.n \wedge v \notin P1.S : ((m, v), to.(m, n))\}$
$\quad \cup \{l, u_0, u_1 : (u_0, u_1) \in R0.m \wedge l \in P1.V \wedge u_0, u_1 \notin P0.S : ((u_0, l), (u_1, l))\}$
$\quad \cup \{v_0, v_1 : (v_0, v_1) \in R1.n \wedge v_0, v_1 \notin P1.S : ((m, v_0), (m, v_1))\}$
$\quad \cup \{l, u, v : (u, to.m) \in R0.m \wedge (from.l, v) \in R1.n \wedge u \notin P0.S \wedge v \notin P1.S :$
$\qquad\qquad\qquad\qquad\qquad\qquad\qquad\qquad\qquad ((u, l), (m, v))\}$
$\quad \cup \{k, l : ((from.k, to.m) \in R0.m \wedge l = n) \vee ((from.l, to.n) \in R1.n \wedge k = m) :$
$\qquad\qquad\qquad\qquad\qquad\qquad\qquad\qquad (from.(k, l), to.(m, n))\}$,

for all $m \in P0.V$ and $n \in P1.V$.

Next we consider the construction of a deadlock-free routing algorithm for P. We start by investigating the cyclicity of R. As can easily be verified we have that R is acyclic iff both $R0$ and $R1$ are acyclic. If R is acyclic then according to theorem 7.7, R is deadlock-free. From now on we assume that R is cyclic. Let P' be the virtual processor network associated with P. Suppose that $P0'$ has routing algorithm $R0'$

induced by $R0$ and $<_0$, and similarly for $P1'$. For elements $((u_0, l), (u_1, l))$ of R we define the relation $<$ on $P.E$ by

$$(u_0, l) < (u_1, l) \equiv u_0 <_0 u_1 .$$

Similarly for elements $((m, v_0), (m, v_1))$ of R

$$(m, v_0) < (m, v_1) \equiv v_0 <_1 v_1 .$$

For the remaining elements of R, $((u, l), (m, v))$ with $(u, to.m) \in R0.m$, $(from.l, v) \in R1.n$, $u \notin P0.S$, and $v \notin P1.S$, we observe that once a message is on an edge (m, v), routing is restricted to such edges. This restriction offers the possibility of defining R' induced by R and $<$ on P' in a slightly different way than in the definition of the previous section.

Routing algorithm R' induced by R and $<$ on P' is the routing algorithm that for all $k, l, m, n \in P'.V$, $w_0, w_1 \in (P0.E - P0.S) \times P1.V$ or $w_0, w_1 \in P0.V \times (P1.E - P1.S)$, $u \in (P0.E - P0.S) \times P1.V$, $v \in P0.V \times (P1.E - P1.S)$, $w \in P.E - P.S$, and $i \geq 0$ satisfies:

- $(from.(k, l), (w, i)) \in R'.(m, n) \quad \equiv \quad (from.(k, l), w) \in R.(m, n) \wedge i = 0,$
- $((w, i), to.(m, n)) \in R'.(m, n) \quad \equiv \quad (w, to.(m, n)) \in R.(m, n),$
- $((w_0, i), (w_1, i)) \in R'.(m, n) \quad \equiv \quad (w_0, w_1) \in R.(m, n) \wedge w_0 < w_1,$
- $((w_0, i), (w_1, i + 1)) \in R'.(m, n) \quad \equiv \quad (w_0, w_1) \in R.(m, n) \wedge \neg(w_0 < w_1),$
- $(((u, l), i), ((m, v), 0)) \in R'.(m, n) \quad \equiv \quad ((u, l), (m, v)) \in R.(m, n),$
- $(from.(k, l), to.(m, n)) \in R'.(m, n) \equiv \quad (from.(k, l), to.(m, n)) \in R.(m, n).$

A proof similar to that of theorem 7.7 can be given to show that R' is acyclic. Hence R' is deadlock-free. It is clear that the number of levels needed in P' equals the maximum of $M0$ and $M1$. Next we give two examples of classes of processor networks to which the method can be applied.

Example 7.11 *boolean n-cube*

The boolean n-cube (see example 2.1) may be regarded as the cartesian product of n copies of the complete network with 2 nodes. According to example 7.9 we conclude that the routing algorithm described above is deadlock-free. It is the E-cube routing algorithm ([Lang82]): a message arriving on edge u with $t.u = k$ destined for node l is routed on the edge corresponding to the position of the most significant bit in which k and l differ.

(End of example)

Example 7.12 k-ary n-cube, $k \geq 3$

The k-ary n-cube (see example 2.1) is a processor network with k^n nodes. Each node has an n-digit radix-k address a and is adjacent to those nodes whose addresses differ from a by 1 in exactly one digit. Notice that a k-ary 1-cube is a ring of k nodes, and a k-ary 2-cube is a torus processor network. Hence, the k-ary n-cube may be regarded as the cartesian product of n copies of the ring network with k nodes. According to example 7.10 the method results in a deadlock-free routing algorithm requiring two levels.

(End of example)

From these two examples we derive an important conclusion. Consider the bidirectional ring network P_b with four vertices. Then we have that P_b is as a graph isomorphic to the boolean 2-cube. According to example 7.10 the standard routing algorithm S for P_b requires two levels, whereas the boolean 2-cube requires only one level for the E-cube routing algorithm. This difference can be explained by observing that the E-cube routing algorithm is deterministic, while S is non-deterministic. Hence restricting the order in which the 'dimensions' are traversed results in deadlock-free routing algorithms with fewer levels. In essence, in the routing algorithm R described above for cartesian product processor networks we have used the same restriction on the order in which the dimensions are traversed. When we describe routing in terms of paths between nodes, then R for $P0 \times P1$ may be interpreted as follows. Let (k, l) and (m, n) be nodes of $P0 \times P1$. Then the path between (k, l) and (m, n) established by R is represented by

(route-in-$P0(k, m), l$) ; (m, (route-in-$P1(l, n)$)) ,

where route-in-$P0(k, m)$ denotes a path in $P0$ from node k to node m, and similarly for $P1$. A consequence of the method presented here is thus that this 'routing algorithm' requires $M0$ **max** $M1$ levels.

This concludes our discussion about deadlock-free routing algorithms.

References

[Aker86] Sheldon B. Akers and Balakrishnan Krishnamurthy,
A group theoretic model for symmetric interconnection networks, in *Proceedings of the 1986 International Conference on Parallel Processing*, 1986, pp. 216–223.

[Anne87] Fred Annexstein, Marc Baumslag and Arnold L. Rosenberg,
Group action graphs and parallel architectures, *COINS Technical Report 87-133*, University of Amherst, 1987.

[Berg73] Claude Berge,
Graphs and Hypergraphs, North-Holland Publishing Company, 1973.

[Berm86] J.-C. Bermond, C. Delorme, and J.-J. Quisquater,
Strategies for interconnection networks: some methods from graph theory, *Journal of Parallel and Distributed Computing*, 1986, pp. 433–449.

[Bodl86] H.L. Bodlaender,
Distributed computing, structure and complexity, Ph.D. Thesis, Utrecht University, 1986.

[Cido87] I. Cidon, J.M. Jaffe, and M. Sidi,
Local distributed deadlock detection by cycle detection and clustering, *IEEE Transactions on Software Engineering*, **SE-13**, No. 1, January 1987.

[Dall86a] William J. Dally and Charles L. Seitz,
Deadlock free message routing in multiprocessor interconnections networks, Dept. Comp. Sc., California Institute of Technology, Tech. Rep. 5206:TR:86.

[Dall86b] William J. Dally and Charles L. Seitz,
The torus routing chip, *Distributed Computing*, **1(4)**, 1986, pp. 187–196.

[Dall89] William J. Dally,
A VLSI architecture for concurrent data structures, Kluwer, Hingham, MA, 1987.

[Desh86] Sanjay R. Deshpande and Roy M. Jenevein,
Scaleability of a binary tree on a hypercube, in *Proceedings of the 1986 International Conference on Parallel Processing*, 1986, pp. 661–668.

[Dijk90] Edsger W. Dijkstra and Carel S. Scholten,
Predicate Calculus and Program Semantics, Springer Verlag, New York, 1990.

[Even79] Shimon Even, *Graph Algorithms*, Computer Science Press, 1979.

[Fish82] John P. Fishburn and Raphael A. Finkel,
Quotient networks, *IEEE Transaction on Computers*, **C-31**, No. 4, 1982,
pp. 288–295.

[Gunt81] Klaus D. Günther,
Prevention of deadlocks in packet-switched data transport systems, *IEEE
Transactions on Communications*, **Com-29**, No.4, April 1981, pp. 512–524.

[Hara69] Frank Harary,
it Graph Theory, Addison-Wesley Publishing Company, 1969.

[Hess86] Wim H. Hesselink and Menno T. Kosters,
Large point-symmetric networks with small diameter and degree, unpub-
lished article, Groningen University, 1986.

[Hilb90] Peter A.J. Hilbers and Johan J. Lukkien,
Deadlock-free message routing in multicomputer networks, *Distributed
Computing*, **4(3)**, 1989, pp. 178–186.

[Ho 87] Ching-Tien Ho and S. Lennart Johnsson,
On the embedding of arbitrary meshes in boolean cubes with expansion
two dilation two, in *Proceedings of the 1987 International Conference on
Parallel Processing* (Sartaj K. Sahni, ed.), 1987, pp. 188–191.

[Lang82] Charles Lang Jr.,
The extension of object-oriented languages to a homogeneous, concurrent
architecture, Dept. Comp. Sc., California Institute of Technology, Tech.
Rep. 5014:TR:82.

[Li 86] Peyyun Peggy Li and Alain J. Martin,
The sneptree – a versatile interconnection network, in *Proceedings of the
1986 International Conference on Parallel Processing*, 1986, pp. 20–27.

[Mart80] Alain J. Martin,
A distributed implementation method for parallel programming, in *Proceedings IFIP Conference 80* (S. H. Lavington, ed.), 1980, pp. 309–314.

[Mart82] Alain J. Martin,
Distributed computations on arrays of processors, it Philips tech. Rev., **40**,
no. 8/9, 1982, pp. 270–277.

[Mart] Alain J. Martin and Jan L.A. van de Snepscheut,
Networks of machines for distributed recursive computations, to appear in
IEEE Transactions on Computers.

[Prep81] Franco P. Preparata and Jean Vuillemin,
The cube connected cycles: a versatile network for parallel computation, *Communications of the ACM*, **24**, no. 5, 1981, pp. 300–309.

[Prep84] Franco P. Preparata,
VLSI algorithms and architectures, in *Proceedings Mathematical Foundations of Computer Science*, Lecture Notes in Computer Science, **176**, Springer-Verlag, 1984, pp. 149–161.

[Rem 79] Martin Rem,
Mathematical aspects of VLSI design, in *Proceedings Caltech Conference on VLSI*, 1979, pp. 55–64.

[Rose84] Arnold L. Rosenberg,
Issues in the study of graph embeddings, in *Graph-Theoretic Concepts in Computer Science* (H. Noltemeier, ed.), Lecture Notes in Computer Science, **100**, Springer-Verlag, 1984, pp. 149–161.

[Seit84] Charles L. Seitz,
Concurrent VLSI architectures, *IEEE Transactions on Computers*, **C-33**, no. 12, 1984, pp. 1247–1265.

[Snep81] Jan L.A. van de Snepscheut,
Mapping a dynamic tree on a fixed graph, private communications JAN78a, 1981.

[Witt81] Larry D. Wittie,
Communication structures for large networks of microcomputers, *IEEE Transactions on Computers*, **C-30**, no. 4, 1981, pp.264–273.

[Woo 89] Jinwoon Woo and Sartaj Sahni,
Hypercube computing: connected components, *The Journal of Supercomputing*, **3**, 1989, pp. 209–234.

[Wu 85] Angela Y. Wu,
Embedding of tree networks into hypercubes, *Journal of Parallel and Distributed Computing*, **2**, 1985, pp. 238–249.

Index

Printed in the United States
By Bookmasters